DATE DUE

ELIZABETH and PHILIP

Elizabeth and Philip

by Geoffrey Bocca

Profusely Illustrated with Photographs

HENRY HOLT *and* **COMPANY** *New York*

ELIZABETH *and* PHILIP

 CHAPTER *ONE*

To the anger of Arabs and other peoples recently liberated from the British, Englishmen in the first year of the reign of Queen Elizabeth II continued to behave like Englishmen just as if nothing had happened.

Spreading across Europe in search of the food they could not get at home and the sunshine which no longer shone on the British Empire, Elizabeth's loyal subjects continued to treat Frenchmen, Italians, and other foreign fellows with a combination of kindness, condescension, and sympathy. They demanded—and usually got—the maximum of service and respect for the seventy dollar yearly allowance permitted them by the British Treasury to spend abroad.

They laughed at the ridiculous amounts of food available in Paris and Rome and thanked God for England and civilization. In England the English way of life disappeared in fits and starts. At times it seemed on the point of death. Then it would get up and thrash about like a wounded whale. Randolph Turpin, a colored Englishman trained on fish and chips, won the world's middleweight championship from Sugar Ray Robinson shortly before the King died,

3

then lost it by an absurd performance a few weeks later in New York.

The stately homes of England remained stately even if they were hardly homes anymore. The London newspapers ran rollicking league tables to see which noble lord was getting the most half crowns from throwing his castle open to the public. (The winner was the Duke of Devonshire whose Derbyshire home, Chatsworth House, during one holiday week end took in 5,716 people; second came the Earl of Harewood with 3,700 people to Harewood House; and third the Marquis of Bath with a round 3,000 to Longleat.)

A few people sighed when Garrard's of Albemarle Street, jewelers to the Royal Family since 1751, bowed before the onward sweep of austerity and shut up shop. The one hundred per cent tax on jewelry and the declining purchasing power of the aristocracy was too much for them. However, the name of the shop together with its patterns and sketches was sold to the Goldsmith's and Silversmith's, a glittering monument on Regent Street to the fact that there were still Englishmen with the money to buy the treasures of the earth.

The British talent for understatement had improved rather than degenerated under the pressure of the times. Seventeen-year-old Dennis Hulbert, by a phenomenal bowling (pitching) performance, enabled Harrow to defeat

4

Eton in the annual cricket match for the first time in years. A scholarship boy, the son of a policeman, Hulbert was cheered all the way to the pavilion at Lords while his schoolmates, scions of the nation's privileged classes, swarmed outside shouting, "Hulbert! Hulbert!"

To a newspaperman Hulbert commented blushingly, "I don't know what all the fuss is about. I'm not very good at cricket. I'm not very good at anything really."

Meanwhile another statement which will be recalled by sports lovers, even after the pomp and ceremony of the Coronation are forgotten, is Tony Cox's superbly British explanation of why he finished last in the single sculls at the Olympic Games at Helsinki. "The start was frightful. Missed my stroke and nearly fell into the water. When I looked round there I was twenty lengths behind. Wasn't a ruddy thing I could do about it."

Despite taxes which sometimes took up to ninety-seven cents in the dollar, a few Englishmen still managed to amass gigantic fortunes. Charles Clore, the wizard of the stock market, made millions on speculations in real estate. Capital gains were his specialty. He would buy property at a low price, then sell when the market was right. As capital gains are untaxed in England (they are taxed at twenty-five per cent in the United States) he pocketed the lot and became England's first postwar millionaire.

Sir Bernard Docker, boss of the Daimler Motor Company, and his wife set out earnestly to spend a million pounds. Among the things he bought his wife was a gold-plated Daimler spangled with 18,000 golden stars. The estimated cost: $45,000. When Lady Docker saw it she is reported to have murmured, "I hope people won't think it vulgar."

Millions were spent on football pools by a nation tormented with the example of a tiny few who had made hundreds of thousands of dollars (untaxed) on the layout of a few pennies. The aim was to guess the results of the hundred or so top soccer games played in England and Scotland every Saturday. The pool promoters all became millionaires.

But a campaign by the Royal Society to raise $710,000 from all over the world to erect a George Bernard Shaw Memorial actually produced less than $3,000.

A lunatic named John Thomas Straffen who had been confined to Broadmoor Prison for the criminal insane because he had killed a child, escaped and killed another, and even a nation notorious for its callousness to children was shocked.

A newspaper voted Winston Churchill's government the best dressed since 1931. The ever-sharp Anthony Eden was at the top of the poll, followed by forty-eight-year-old David Eccles, the Minister of Works, whose bold ties and Edwardian waistcoats commanded admiration. Worst dressed of the lot, said the newspaper coldly, was Dr. Charles Hill, a man who became so famous on the British Broadcasting Corporation as "the Radio Doctor" that he ran for Parliament, as a Conservative, or rather a Liberal National, which is a jocular version of the same animal. Dr. Hill was advised to go home and have his clothes sponged and pressed. Cynics who watched his work in Parliament suggested he should just go home.

Deauville, France, still turned its eyes to Britain's rich to add luster to the season. The first year of Elizabeth's reign found such eminent personalities as the Duke and Duchess of Devonshire, the Earl and Countess of Carnarvon, Denise Lady Newborough, and Captain Cecil Boyd-Rochfort, the Queen's trainer, all there.

To lure still more of the sporting belt, Deauville's hotels chartered an aircraft to pick up the first grouse killed in Scotland on August 12 and fly them in to stiffen the menu.

But the Duke of Sutherland cut his holiday short in spite of the appearance of "*coq de bruyère ecossais*" on the *à la carte*. The Maitre d'Hotel was *un peu* put out at his disappearance, and it was *difficile* to explain to him that the English lord preferred to go home, *chez lui*, and shoot his own grouse.

In London Rosa Lewis died. She was a fabulous Edwardian who ran the Cavendish Hotel in Jermyn Street. As a hotel it lacked many of the comforts appreciated by

Americans, but it was haunted by an air of Edwardian raffishness that attracted the great names of Europe and America. Rosa, close friend of Edward VII, would stand her favorite guests double sherries at odd hours, and as they left they would get bills which bore no relation whatever to the service and accommodation they received. She liked Tennessee Williams so much she took down a valuable picture from the wall as he left and gave it to him. She was eighty-five, and had been eighty-five for years.

And talking about Americans, the tourists occupied London in force. One, in the Dorchester Hotel bar, was heard to say, "These English martinis taste like lemonade," and half an hour later was led shouting to the street. Yet what he said was quite true. The way to give the disgusting English martinis a certain amount of zing was to ask the barman to add a dash, just a dash, of absinthe. This flattened the taste but made them somewhat atomic. Two was the recommended limit for those who did not want to find themselves lying helplessly on their backs with their arms flailing.

Lady Aberconway judged a contest for "the deportment of cats on leads." She enumerated her principles. "I have always detested cats on leads," she said. "They are such independent creatures. I shall look for a cat that is happy on its lead and is not dragged behind its mistress."

Cats reminded a certain South African gentleman of

kippers. Showing a total lack of *sang-froid* when face to face with English food, Major Hubert Juta went back to Johannesburg saying, "Breakfast, bah! You get a choice of kipper, haddock, fried cod, or fish cakes. I'm sorry, but the English breakfast proved too much of a strain."

"Kippers!" commented the elderly English gentleman in the Ritz Hotel, expertly boning the delicacy at eight A.M. while his mouth watered and his eyes gleamed. "The fellow's mad. What's wrong with kippers?"

Burke's Landed Gentry—the official and exclusive caste list of the land-owning classes—was falling on bad days. Landed gentry are now so scarce that the publishers had to scrabble round for enough names to fill the 1952 edition, the first since 1939. Space was even found for film stars, novelists, and similar dubious possessors of land and talent.

West End critics gave Sir Ralph Richardson one of the worst roastings in living memory for his performance as Macbeth at the Stratford-on-Avon Festival. Actors all over the country were beginning to seethe at the sharpness of the critics. Trouble was that in the small London papers the critics were only being allowed three or four paragraphs for each show, and they were finding the space just right for the witty epigram and the killing phrase, but not for anything more detailed.

The Evening Standard critic Kenneth Tynan (author

9

of such unkind cuts as the describing of a well-known London actress as "spectacularly miscast as the toast of two continents"), was particularly disliked. Actors waited hopefully for one of their number to flatten the detestable Tynan with a blow, but he continued to thrive, literate and devastating, and one elderly actress in the Marquess of Granby tavern in Cambridge Circus was heard to exclaim, "It's terrible! It's a free country, isn't it? Why don't they stop him writing such things?"

Theatergoing in London was an exciting business. Audiences hissed and booed the plays they didn't like, and one author of a particularly bad play so narrowly escaped being beaten up by a couple of critics that he threw a police cordon round the theater on the second (and last) performance.

England was beginning to win again at sports. For one thing, the cricket authorities had abandoned the snobbish old tradition of having the England cricket team captained by an amateur. The country's first professional captain, a tough, broken-nosed Yorkshireman named Len Hutton, led England to an overwhelming and ruthless victory over India in the Test Matches, which are the equivalent of America's World Series.

In 1953 the all-important Australian cricket team was due to arrive for five Test Matches and England entertained real hopes of winning the rubber for the first time since

1932. Hutton's startlingly optimistic forecast was, "We'll win every game," and Englishmen liked to think that Down Under the Australians were quaking in their shoes.

England kept on whacking the Continentals at soccer, and the first Epsom Derby of Elizabeth's reign was won by the British-bred horse, Tulyar, against French competition which had dominated the Derby ever since the end of World War II, and was expected to dominate it again in 1952. This was the nicest gift that anyone could present to the Queen, who has a passion for horse racing; and if Tulyar's victory could not be considered more than coincidental with her accession, it was also symbolic.

English women golfers won the Curtis Cup from the United States for the first time, and in the Olympic Games the British did not do too badly.

Politically the nation hopped from crisis to crisis. The Conservatives worked doggedly to achieve peace on the one hand and prosperity on the other—to the ribald jeers of the Labor Opposition. These jeers they had learned from the Conservatives who, when they were in Opposition, jeered the identical measures which the Labor government had taken to face identical crises.

Britons continued to grumble outrageously, dress elegantly, face the future calmly (or apathetically, depending whether the observer is an Anglophile or an Anglophobe), eat badly, breed with purity, keep warm in cold houses, and fit snugly into automobiles designed for a large dog or small man.

High and low, Englishmen, Scotsmen, Welshmen, and certain breeds of Irishmen (not limited to the North), they were the Queen's men. They held for the young Elizabeth probably the greatest passion any British monarch had enjoyed since the days of Elizabeth I. They were a formidable force, these Britons, not always lovable, not always even nice, but always a source of influence and power. The time unfortunately could not be too far away when the Queen would have to do without Winston Churchill. The great man is enormously old and his resources are dwindling. There are old men in England today who cannot remember a time when Churchill was not a personality and a power in the land.

After Churchill goes, all sorts of new Elizabethan influences will be needed to bridge the almost unimaginable gap. She might look to the confident Anthony Eden, or to the trusted Clement Attlee whose potential of both strength and weakness can never be accurately estimated even by the sharpest of observers. Or she might be obliged to turn to Aneurin Bevan, the wild Welshman whose Celtic fire is so profoundly distrusted by the more phlegmatic English.

If the thought is disturbing, there is another aspect to it. The Queen is as tough as Aneurin Bevan any day of the week. She has an infinite capacity to be what the English beautifully describe as "bloody-minded," which is a stronger word for obstinate. She needs to be with subjects who are both fiercely loyal and "bloody-minded" themselves.

In the summer of 1952 the Scots were trying hard to insist that she was Elizabeth *the First* of Scotland, as they never had much use for the first Elizabeth. The Scottish Communists have tried to make a burning issue of it. More respectable spokesmen like the Lord Provost of Edinburgh and *The Scotsman* newspaper have tried to suggest deferentially the justice of the Scottish argument. Queen Elizabeth has been moved as little by the one as by the other.

A few months after she became Queen, she had to attend a function in Scotland and found that a ceremonial cup which she had to present, was inscribed "Queen Elizabeth," and butter not melting in the mouths of the local officials. Ruthlessly ignoring their protestations of innocence, she had the cup sent back for the "II" to be added to her name.

It was all in the family. Whatever the future of the British Empire, Queen Elizabeth commanded a spontaneous devotion that no Hitler or Stalin could hope for. England, underfed and swept by the cold winds that seeped even into the sitting rooms, was still the Mecca of Englishmen everywhere. It tugged at the emotions of New Zealanders, Australians, South Africans, and Canadians; and the influx of young Dominions citizens, particularly those interested in the arts and letters, into London in the postwar years positively embarrassed the Dominions Office which would have preferred the movement to be outgoing from the over-crowded island.

There was nothing to be done about it. Ask the English actors like Clive Brook, Ian Hunter, and Laurence Olivier who basked for years in the golden glory of California, but were somehow sucked back to England and all its discomforts.

Here was the one great Third Force in the world, a balance and a check to the powers of Soviet Russia and free America, and it all revolved round a girl of twenty-five.

 CHAPTER *TWO*

Princess Elizabeth of England and Prince Philip of Greece had known each other since childhood, and loved each other since 1944, but it was not until September, 1945, when they were approximately 12,000 miles away from each other that the legend began to form.

Close observers put the exact date at VJ Day. The war was over. The Mall, outside Buckingham Palace, was black with cheering people. The Palace itself was floodlit, and time after time the Royal Family appeared on the balcony to acknowledge the roars of their subjects.

At a certain point in the evening, Princess Elizabeth and Princess Margaret, then aged nineteen and fifteen respectively, slipped away to join the crowds. It was obviously impossible to escape unnoticed by the front entrance so they left by one of the side doors, near Victoria Station. They were not alone. Apart from the detectives who kept as remote as security and as close as discretion would allow, they were also escorted by a band of young men in the uniform of the Guards or the Royal Navy—somehow the aristocracy in Britain has usually kept slightly aloof from the more bourgeois atmosphere of the Royal Air Force.

The men were tall, thin, and as pale as young men must be who have spearheaded a long and exhausting war. Most of them were fair. There was a slight tendency toward receding chins, and here and there a touch of sartorial refinement for which Englishmen, even in uniform, have a positive genius. One or two wore suède shoes. Their socks and ties were lemon colored. Some wore the ribbons of the D.S.O., M.C., and D.S.C.

The girls wore the starkly simple suits that were the cross that English girls had to bear through the war years. In a compact convoy of cars they snaked cautiously through the dark and battered London streets watching the fringes of the bedlam that roared and crackled all over the West End. Piccadilly and the Circus were jammed with people and totally inaccessible. Some revelers had started a huge bonfire in the Haymarket with junk from bomb sites. But Mayfair, Covent Garden, and parts of Soho were still open to traffic.

After a long tour the party ended at the Dorchester, the Park Lane hotel which managed to stay smart and exclusive throughout the war. They took a table in a quiet corner of the ballroom and ordered a bottle of champagne. Everybody who saw the party that night agreed on one thing, the quietness of it all; so unlike the hearty dinner and

16

night club sessions which both Elizabeth and Margaret were to throw a few years later.

It was not hard to understand the reason. Princess Elizabeth, a gay and ebullient girl in spite of her persistent reputation as "the quiet one" of the two Royal sisters, had little to say, and her companions inherited her mood. Already circles close to the British court knew that the relationship between Elizabeth and Prince Philip of Greece was very serious indeed.

Philip was not in the party. Almost at that moment he was sailing into Tokyo Bay, a lieutenant in the destroyer HMS *Whelp*, after a rigorous and almost nonstop war in the Mediterranean and the Pacific Ocean. Elizabeth had not seen him in almost a year.

Unlike Princess Margaret, whose dates and apparently endless roster of boy friends were later to charm and intrigue the world, Princess Elizabeth was a one-man girl, and her friends knew it. Yet it was a strange affair, and it would have been possible to have named half a dozen young men with whom Elizabeth could have made a more obvious match. Philip was different from other young men in British high society. He was tougher. He was more democratic. He had knocked about the world. He preferred pubs to cocktail bars. He had a passion for physical fitness. He played all sports better than most. He did not get a "correct" education. In all ways he failed to fit into the mold.

When Elizabeth was a very small girl she asked King George V, her grandfather, "When I get married, Grandpapa, will I have to marry Royalty?" The old King laughed heartily and told the conversation to his wife, Queen Mary. At once the Queen jotted down a list of the small boys who would one day be eligible for Elizabeth's hand, and she discussed the list with an intimate friend.

The list was remarkably accurate. It included nearly all the close friends whom Elizabeth acquired as she grew up. But it did not include Prince Philip of Greece.

During the war when it became plain that the only person Elizabeth ever thought of was the person Queen Mary forgot, King George VI, Queen Elizabeth, and the old Queen Mother had moments of anxiety. Philip, after all, had no money. His parents were separated and both were in territories occupied by the Germans. During his brief period in power in Greece, Philip's father, Prince Andrew, was involved in an administration so futile that he had actually to be rescued by the Royal Navy from condign punishment at the hands of Greek revolutionaries. The husbands of Philip's three surviving sisters were fighting for the Nazis.

But Philip won the Royal Family over. His birth was acceptable from the start. Like Elizabeth he was a great-grandson of Queen Victoria, and the two were second cousins. He was, of course, Greek only by title. His grandmother was the first Marchioness of Milford Haven, married to Prince Louis of Battenberg, a German noble who became a British citizen before World War I. Lord Louis Mountbatten was one of the sons of this marriage, and so was Princess Alice, Philip's mother. Philip's father, Prince Andrew, was Danish. Philip left Greece at the age of twelve months and for most of his life he had lived as an Englishman. He still carried a Greek passport but that, too, was accidental. He planned to apply for British citizenship in 1939, but the war intervened.

Of all the Royal Family, Queen Mary became possibly his greatest fan. Philip, with his fair hair and blue eyes, reminded her of her own children.

The relationship and apparent course of Elizabeth's and Philip's relationship became accepted at Buckingham Palace, but Queen Mary's list of eligibles was revived during the war for quite the opposite reason from that for which she first intended it. This time some of the King's advisers, including Mr. Churchill, feared that Philip, in the front line of naval service, might be killed. Knowing Elizabeth's feelings, court circles started to get agitated. Other eligible young officers, as soon as they drifted home on leave, were promptly collared and invited to Windsor where Elizabeth was staying. It was hoped that Elizabeth's interests might widen, and, if the worst should happen, she would have other friends who could offer some degree of consolation.

The worst never happened. Philip, like most carefree people, was born lucky. At the end of the war he found himself with a string of campaign ribbons and a "Mentioned-in-Despatches." He was unscratched and untouched by even a trace of the fevers that came to servicemen from the Middle and Far East.

But on the day of the celebration he was at the other end of the globe and not due back for many months to come, and the VJ Day party was a quiet one. Elizabeth, like thousands and millions of girls all over the world, was thinking of the release from tension, and of the future that she could now face squarely and with confidence. In normal times a princess' life is a good life. Unfortunately for Elizabeth, the years which are normally the years of most pleasure—the coming-of-age and the debutante days—were spent in the war and at war work.

The others at the party chattered among themselves, respecting her preoccupation. But anyone who took his mind off the world situation for one moment could see that a new era was about to begin. The British Royal Family was about to take a unique position in the world. And the center of the family was not the King, in spite of his position, nor Princess Margaret, for all her glamour and pranks.

It was Elizabeth, the girl who would one day become Queen of England. Her ideas and her friends, her choice of clothes and her choice of husband were not only interesting, they were of world-wide importance. This party was the dividing line between the wartime Royal Family, hardworking, self-effacing, and obscured by security censorship, and the postwar Royal Family which was about to attract publicity and attention such as none of the stars of Hollywood had ever dreamed of.

Elizabeth had already started to have a good time. Her party at the Dorchester was an inauspicious introduction to the night life of London, but a few weeks earlier she had been to the Derby and to Ascot. Elizabeth was and is horse-mad, and those visits began what is now turning into a national passion for the turf. A couple of weeks after Ascot Elizabeth was thrown heavily from a horse she was trying out in the grounds at Balmoral. It was the second time in her life she had taken a bad tumble, the first time being in 1937 when she was twelve. On this occasion she was badly bruised about the ribs and legs, but next day she was back on the horse.

After VJ Day Britain settled down to think about economic recovery (she is still thinking about it), and the young British aristocrats began to trickle back from the war fronts. Philip's return was slow. Other young men, some married, some unmarried, who would normally have been seen around the court, did not return at all. The Marquess of Hartington, married to one of the former U. S. Ambassador Joseph Kennedy's daughters, had been killed in the Normandy invasion. The Earl of Aylesford died at Dunkirk. Lord Alington was killed in the Royal Air Force, and Lord Baybrooke of the Guards was killed in North Africa in 1943. They were only a few of the total. The war thinned out British society even more drastically than other societies because so many young nobles were in the country's crack regiments.

Others returned, however, determined to get as much fun out of life as they could after six years at war. The young men later to be seen in the company of Princess Margaret all turned up—the Marquess of Milford Haven, Prince Philip's cousin, back from the Royal Navy; the Marquess of Blandford known as "Sunny," from the Guards; Lord Ogilvy, the Honorable Tom Egerton, the Earl of Dalkeith, and the great favorite of both Elizabeth and Margaret, "Porchie," Lord Porchester. Porchie was unable to entertain Royalty in the manner that the others did because his father, the Earl of Carnarvon, once husband of Tillie Losch, the dancer, was divorced and his family seat had no hostess.

And there were the young men, like Mark Bonham-Carter, whom a benevolent War Office had stationed at Windsor Castle during the war, after a particularly long or trying term of overseas service. Part of the "rest cure" of those days, remembered gratefully by the young officers long after they had returned to civilian life, had been informal, regular family luncheon with the two princesses— and their parents if they were not in London. Friendships made between the two girls and the war-weary youngsters from the desert or battlefields of France and Italy were not easily broken.

Elizabeth was seen with them all at race meetings, theaters, and country outings, but always in parties so impersonal that even the most lynx-eyed of London's gossip writers could see no possible "link."

First reports of a possible engagement between Princess Elizabeth and Prince Philip leaked out in Athens in 1945, even before Philip had returned from Japan. The newspapers became suddenly full of forecasts of a new connection between the British and Greek Royal Households.

Buckingham Palace immediately denied the reports. When they persisted the Palace kept on denying them. Altogether five distinct denials were issued in the eighteen months following VJ Day. But the British and American people, primed by such eager guardians of modern civilization as newspaper photographers, press agents, and gossip columnists, were not so easily fooled. From 1945 the public was convinced that Elizabeth would marry Philip, for the good reason that she was obviously not interested in anyone else whatever.

This was the heyday of the British Labor government and a few Socialists grumbled about the nonsense of it all. A few people, not Socialists, worried about their darling child marrying a foreign prince. But that did not last for long. What was more important was the character of the Prince himself.

As a Cockney taxi driver said to one of his fares whom he recognized as one of Britain's best-known young peers, " 'Oo the 'ell is Prince Philip anyway?"

The peer was in too much of a hurry to stop and tell him. This was something of a pity because the cabbie might have heard a fascinating story.

 CHAPTER *THREE*

When Queen Victoria sprinkled her children and grandchildren around the thrones of Europe, political observers of the day generally credited her with having a lot on the ball. And so she may have had if World War I had not come along to destroy the only kind of world which kings and statesmen then understood.

By 1920, when Queen Victoria was beyond the blandishments of impoverished relatives, the power of international monarchy had dwindled and there were more of Victoria's progeny left stranded in the capitals of the world than the market could absorb.

Glucksburgs were running restaurants in Paris, Hapsburgs modeled in London and New York. Bourbons had a dash at the moving pictures in Hollywood, California, Romanoffs drank tea from samovars in Monte Carlo, and Mr. Cholly Knickerbocker, later on, did a roaring trade in Hohenzollerns.

Of all the royal houses remaining in Europe, the Greek monarchy seemed the most constantly insecure, and it was in the twilight of one of the ephemeral Greek reigns that Prince Philip of Greece and Denmark was born at *"Mon*

Répos," summer home of Prince Andrew and Princess Alice of Greece, on the island of Corfu. The date was June 10, 1921. Philip was a Schleswig-Holstein-Sonderburg-Glucksburg.

The family was Danish with no feelings toward Greece except that universal call which takes a man anyplace where he can find a job. Denmark had been something of a farm system for Greek kings ever since 1863. In 1913 King George I of Greece had been assassinated. Prince Andrew was his fourth son. Andrew married Princess Alice of Battenburg, sister of the present Earl Mountbatten, and the baby, Philip, became sixth in line to the throne of Greece.

The situation in Greece was chaotic. Tension with the Turks was getting more and more intense, and a revolutionary movement in the country itself threatened to overthrow the government. Even while the infant Philip was being baptized in the Greek Orthodox Church, he seemed destined by all the stars, and particularly by the fading star of Greece, to be certain in the near future to join the large fraternity of homeless and impoverished princelings.

His contact with Greece was soon over. By the time he was twelve months old, a chubby child with fair hair and blue eyes, he was on his way by Royal Naval warship to England. His father, holding a command in the Greek Army, had been captured by the revolutionaries, and they were deciding whether to kill him or kick him out of the country.

Eventually they decided on the latter, and another British warship arrived to take the embittered Prince Andrew into exile.

The family escaped with almost nothing. One thing alone saved the baby Prince from complete poverty. This was the care and affection of the powerful English branch of his family. His grandmother, the first Marchioness of Milford Haven, adored him. So did his uncle, Lord Louis Mountbatten. Two years before Lord Louis had married the lovely and wealthy Lady Edwina Ashley, and Philip's four elder sisters, Margarita, Theodora, Cecile, and Sophie were all present at the wedding. All four girls later married German princes, and one married two.

Lord Louis' love for the boy, at first avuncular, became more fatherlike as the years passed. This coming-together was almost inevitable, as Lord Louis never produced a son of his own; and the ties between Philip and his parents became slacker and slacker until in the end they fell apart altogether.

Young Philip spent his first years not only without a home but without a country. A planless, homeless, poverty-dogged, and—for his parents—hopeless decade was to leave on Philip a psychological imprint that was to shape his life. By some happy strength of personality these early years, which might have made him shiftless, were actually to turn him into a man of exceptional character.

Other young princes in the same boat became politically reactionary and joined the *Wehrmacht*. Others held up bars all the way from Vienna to Los Angeles. Others became minor confidence tricksters in order to live the life they enjoyed. They made bad marriages, turned into nasty individuals, and contributed nothing to their children except an inherited title. How different Philip was can be seen today by the man himself.

He was a happy-go-lucky child. At the age of seven he found himself in Paris after having lived already on Corfu and in England. His parents settled down for the time being in a small house outside the city. Philip was old enough now to catch the flair and atmosphere of Paris, and he was never to lose a slightly Gallic touch in his human relations.

Princess Alice enrolled him in a small American school in St. Cloud, a Parisian suburb, and one of the first things he learned was the correct way to swing a baseball bat. At his first try he clipped a small Austrian pupil on the head with punishing force. American children corrected his play and pointed out that the game was played with a ball and not with human skulls. Philip listened with interest and started hitting softballs instead of boys.

Of those early years, and right up to the age of fifteen,

all people who ever came in contact with Philip were impressed with his passion and determination at sports. Competitions and games lured him from whatever else he was doing. He played baseball, cricket, and soccer. He hurdled, ran, climbed, and one teacher can recall him winning a biscuit-eating contest by mouthfuls.

Today, recollections of Philip are tinged with a ghostlike quality. Pictures of the little boy then are startling in their resemblance to someone else. In 1951 a distant relative saw, for the first time, Prince Charles, son of the present Queen Elizabeth and the Duke of Edinburgh.

"Charles!" he cried. "No. It's Philip!"

His amazement was justified. The little boy Charles in every look, from the shaggy blond hair, keen blue eyes, and friendly pout to the big grin and the enthusiastic gesture reminds old friends of the little boy Philip.

The days at St. Cloud were happy ones for Philip even though he lacked certain of the freedoms of the other children. For one thing other boys' parents generally had more money than Philip's, and he had to be very careful with the knees of his heavy tweed knickerbockers. A tumble on the gravel was a serious business for him, and one which took away a lot of his good spirits.

Princess Alice used to sigh when the grubby little urchin, sixth in succession to the nonexistent throne of Greece, came home in the evening. "I'm afraid he will have to make his own way in life," she said to friends. "But I do hope he can grow up in England or America or even Australia, some English-speaking country." At these words Prince Andrew would stare gloomily into the fire and say nothing. He and his wife were finding themselves with progressively less to say to each other.

Philip was old enough to appreciate his comic-opera existence. He knew the realities of life. One friend, visiting Princess Alice for tea, made a laughing comment when she saw the little boy clear away the dishes, ignoring the protests of the maid. "I might have to be a waiter one day," he explained cheerfully.

Some time ago one of the schoolteachers at St. Cloud told a newspaper of her first meeting with Prince Philip. She was Miss Catherine Lewitsky and she went to the school as a junior teacher. She asked each of the twelve boys in the class to introduce himself, so that she would remember them in the future. One dark little boy introduced himself as Wellington Koo. He was the son of the one-time Chinese ambassador to the United States and Britain.

When she asked the fair-haired boy his name, he replied, "Philip."

"Philip what?" she asked.

"Just Philip," said the little boy, shrugging with some embarrassment.

"But you must have another name."

The boy went pink. "Philip of Greece," he replied.

This later became quite a "line" with Philip, particularly when he was talking with girls. Several have gone through the "Philip-what?-Just-Philip" routine, including the daughter of Cobina Wright, the Hollywood columnist. Miss Wright in a recent book tells of a lightweight romance which Philip and the young Miss Wright had just before World War II in France, Philip introducing himself as "Just Philip," leaving the wide-eyed Hollywood deb to find out later that he was a real live prince.

Miss Lewitsky recalled that despite Philip's diffidence at that encounter, he was confident and authoritative, though fair, in his dealings with other children. He blandly made himself monitor of the class and assumed leadership automatically in any schoolboy adventure.

Altogether he spent two years at St. Cloud, after which there was more trouble for the footloose family and it was decided to send Philip alone to London where he could be closer to the Marchioness of Milford Haven and Lord Louis Mountbatten.

Philip stayed with the Mountbattens and was sent to a small private school in Cheam, Surrey, a suburban residential area roughly similar to Forest Hills in New York. His rapidly fading knowledge of French stayed with him long enough to win a first prize in French but otherwise his career there was profoundly undistinguished. It was during the Cheam period, however, that he first met Princess Elizabeth.

Reports on the first meeting vary. Some say it was at Buckingham Palace when old George V threw a party for some Royal children. Others say it was at the Mountbattens' place, at Park Lane in Mayfair. Wherever it was they did meet in both places and quite frequently, but always in parties. Neither had any special feelings toward each other because there are never any points in common between an infant girl of six and a harum-scarum young ruffian of eleven. In fact neither Elizabeth nor Philip can remember these meetings at all. The first time they remember seeing each other was at the Coronation in 1937, which was six years later.

The only significance of the meetings was in the minds of the observers of the scene, all of whom were moved, perhaps haunted, at the contemplation of the fate which had taken two descendants of Queen Victoria along such different roads.

On the one hand there was a graceful, shy little girl of six, clutching the hand of her blue-eyed two-year-old sister. They were the darlings of an Empire, children of the Duke and Duchess of York, and part of the most secure Royal tradition on earth. They had no worries, enemies, doubts, or uncertainties about their future. They did not know what money looked like because everything was taken care of.

On the other side there was Philip, literally a Royal waif-and-stray. His clothes were bought by his grandmother. His father was broke and mooning his life away on the Continent dreaming of the past. Philip did not have a home. Philip's English accent was as pure as Elizabeth's, but he also knew the slang of the streets.

He did not stay in England long. Soon the sliding fortunes of his parents necessitated another move for him. This was an important one, and it took him to Germany. Philip was considerably younger than his four sisters, and all were now married and lived in Germany. Princess Theodora, fifteen years older than Philip, was the second eldest, after Margarita, in the family, and was married to that rare creature, an amiable and liberal-minded German noble, Prince Berthold of Baden. Both of them had become worried at the aimless nature of Philip's upbringing and sent for him. They had a plan.

Both Theodora and Berthold were deeply impressed at the time by the educational theories of Kurt Hahn. Hahn, a German-born graduate of Oxford University, believed that "the sons of the powerful should be emancipated from the prison of privilege." He aimed to achieve this with a school curriculum which combined spartanism and the rigor of a reform school and an advanced study of the humanities.

Berthold offered Hahn his great castle on the shores of Lake Constance at Baden as a testing ground for his theories, and it was to this school, named "Salem," that Philip now came. By now his last frail ties with his parents had shattered. His mother was about to return to Greece while his father continued to wander morosely between Monte Carlo and Paris.

For the next few years Hahn was to become the greatest influence on Philip's life. In fact much of Philip's outlook today is still molded from the teachings of Hahn, and he is passing a good deal of it on to Prince Charles. The hundred or so boys, mostly sons of the German aristocracy, under Hahn's tutelage learned to be tough and self-reliant. They climbed mountains, made boats, and slept under the stars. For a while the life was ideal, but it did not last very long.

The Nazis came to power in 1933, and Philip watched the Brown Shirts march through Baden. Prince Berthold was not a Nazi, and as he was the most important man in Baden he succeeded for some time in keeping Hahn's school outside of Nazi control.

It was not easy, and Philip became a definite worry. Although the young Prince with his Nordic blood, blue eyes, and blond hair was, physically, everything to delight

34

a Nazi philosopher, his character was not. Philip was twelve and he had spent too long a time in the free, easy, and—in the end—superior way of life of France and England to be receptive to the German strutting. Every time he saw a Hitler salute he got an uncontrollable attack of the giggles. Once Theodora's butler caught the alarming sight of Philip swaggering after a band of Nazi soldiers with an uproarious imitation of the German goose-step. The butler hastily snatched Philip up and took the indignant young man to safety.

Hahn's teaching made his pupils react in different ways to the rise of Hitler. Many graduated from the spartan life to become *Wehrmacht* officers. Others, like Philip, revolted from the brake which the Nazis put on their liberty. Hahn, along with Berthold, did his best to keep the school away from the Nazi attention, but he could not keep it up. The tough, hard-bitten boys were too obvious raw material for the Germans. The Nazis learned that Hahn was partly Jewish and threw him into prison on the excuse (it was as good as any other) that he was a Communist. For another year Berthold tried to keep the school alive, but when Hahn was released the two men agreed that it was better to get out while the getting was good. Hahn packed and arranged to take the school to England, and Philip got ready—once more—to find a new home.

Theodora wept when she saw her young brother off

at Baden station. There was good reason for tears. Already, wise men in Germany could see what kind of trouble was brewing. Theodora and Berthold knew that Philip was not only going out of their lives but might one day be trying to kill them.

In World War II the worst came true and no family in the world was more completely shattered. Prince Berthold fought in the *Wehrmacht*. So did Prince Gottfried of Hohenlohe-Langenberg, husband of Princess Margarita. Prince Christopher of Hesse, husband of Princess Sophie, was killed while serving as a major in the *Luftwaffe* in Italy at a time when Prince Philip was serving in the Royal Navy in the Mediterranean (in 1946 Sophie married Prince George of Hanover and they now live in Athens). Princess Cecile and her husband were both killed in an air crash in 1937. Philip's mother, Princess Alice, spent the war in holy orders in Greece while the Germans were in occupation, and Philip's father went on drifting around Monte Carlo and Pétainist France until he died in 1944.

Influential friends helped Kurt Hahn to resume in Britain where he had left off in Germany. Among them were Lord Tweedsmuir, formerly John Buchan the novelist; and Admiral Sir Herbert Richmond, Master of Downing College, Cambridge. While Hahn scouted round England and Scotland for a new site for his school, Philip stayed either with the old Marchioness of Milford Haven or with the Mountbattens in London. Philip was, in effect, an orphan and Lord Louis became his father in all but name. From Lord Louis, Philip began to acquire such Mountbatten characteristics as a love for the sea, and a political awareness greater than that held by most boys of thirteen.

He met Elizabeth and Margaret again. On Philip's side there was still no signs of any great esteem for the little Princess, now aged eight. Elizabeth and Margaret usually played with the Mountbattens' two daughters, and four small girls were a formidable weight for a boy like Philip. It is very probable in fact, knowing Philip's exceptional knowledge of the world at this time that four little girls all sheltered from contact with the outside world must have looked as identical as Chinese and all equally insufferable.

Philip, with his antics, always gave the girls a good time. Elizabeth and another girl screamed with laughter when Philip took control of the fast American-built elevator in the Mountbattens' new penthouse in Chester Street, Mayfair, and propelled it up and down at top speed. The Buckingham Palace elevators were, and are, snail-like, and the Prince and the Princess played with the Mountbattens' express for hours. A couple of days later a guest was halfway to the second floor when the elevator broke down, and the trapped guest blasphemed helplessly until workmen came to repair it.

37

At the wedding of Philip's cousin Marina to the Duke of Kent, Elizabeth met him again. Elizabeth was a bridesmaid and Philip a page. Later they met at Coppins, the Buckinghamshire home of the Kents.

It is very likely that at this point Lord Louis Mountbatten began to see for the first time the advantages in a future marriage between Elizabeth and Philip.

At last from Kurt Hahn, the seventy-odd boys left in his school heard the good word. He had found the place he wanted to reopen Salem. It was an ancient house in Gordonstoun, near Elgin, in the North of Scotland, near Hopeman Bay. Once upon a time the house had belonged to the Red Comyn, a historic murderer from the Orson Welles period of Scottish history.

Here was everything to appeal to boys of hardihood and adventure. It was a part of the world where the summer is watery and the winter winds are freezing. Wet mists eat into the bones. The fishermen of the district are dour and speak a Scots dialect so broad that it often has to be translated for visitors from England. The seas are rough and the life is hard. Elgin itself is a pretty and historic little town, but the nearest metropolitan civilization is in Inverness, several hours away by bus.

This was heaven for Philip. With some of Hahn's other students, he outfitted a cutter which they sailed through the roaring North Sea and along the Scottish coast.

During the first voyage every boy in the boat except Philip was seasick in one degree or another. As Philip was the only one with a stomach strong enough to endure the fumes and odors of the galley, he was made ship's cook and set about industriously making meals for the rest of the crew.

It was debatable whether the galley smells grew better or worse after Philip started work. Some years later one of Philip's shipmates was asked over lunch what kind of dishes Philip served. A most extraordinary expression crossed his face. He laid down his knife and fork and said, "A sort of stew."

"Is that all?" he was asked.

"That's all," he replied and resumed his lunch with a manner indicating unmistakably that the subject was to be changed.

In every way Gordonstoun was superior to Baden. Here Philip could indulge in his passion for the sea as much as he wanted, and under the testing conditions he most enjoyed. Always the kindly, balding Kurt Hahn was there to encourage him in self-reliance, individuality, and force of character. Philip in his small boat explored every bay and creek along that part of the Scottish coast that his Viking ancestors had invaded centuries before. Often he went on all-night fishing trips with the Scottish fishermen who put to sea almost regardless of the weather conditions. He fished and swam, sailed, sculled, and practiced his diving in the

39

freezing water. Soon everyone in the village came to know him, though whether he relished their description of him as "the Greek laddie" is highly doubtful. By now Philip was utterly British and even forgetting his French faster than his teachers were getting it into him. He had never learned to speak Greek. His German was quite nimble and his English was affected only with the slight lilt which comes to anyone exposed for a long time to the burr of the Scot. He occasionally used the ubiquitous Scottish adjective "wee," on occasions like "I'm going to take the wee boat out now," and "How about a wee cup of tea?"

The letters he received showed the scattered nature of his home and family, and the stamps were in great demand among his schoolmates. His mother wrote from Greece. His father wrote from Monte Carlo. His grandmother Lady Milford Haven wrote from London. His sisters wrote from Germany. His uncle Lord Louis Mountbatten, able without strain to compartmentalize his life with cool detachment into (a) playboy, (b) naval officer extraordinary, and (c) statesman, wrote from wherever life took him and his wife: from London, Paris, Vienna, the Riviera, Rome, North Africa.

Philip's replies were spasmodic. He was always a deplorable correspondent. Only in later years when he corresponded with Elizabeth did he show any eagerness to sit down and write letters.

This was the happiest period of Philip's boyhood. Once some female cousins turned up to take Philip off in their car on vacation. Most of the boys had already gone on holiday, but a few were sporting by the fishing boats and along the beach. None was remotely recognizable as Prince Philip of Greece.

Diffidently one of the girls approached a grizzled old salt smoking on the pier and asked if he knew Philip. The answer was a stony "Aye." When the cousin asked where he was to be found the fisherman pointed with his clay pipe. What the horrified cousins saw was a tall but almost unrecognizable boy covered in mud and slime, scraping barnacles off the bottom of a boat and on to himself. Philip, according to one account, was so encrusted in barnacles he gave off sparks when he walked.

The year 1937 was the year of the Coronation of King George VI. Philip had been at Gordonstoun for nearly three years and was now looking forward to the life beyond. He made the trip to London to attend the ceremony, and by that time he had quite definitely decided on a naval career. He was nearly six feet tall, sixteen years old, less beautiful than he had been as a child, and less handsome than he was to become as a man. He was as hard as nails, captain of his school cricket and field hockey teams, and a passable scholar.

Contemporaries have admitted recently that in spite

of Philip's family connections, quite a few eyebrows were raised among the spotty-faced schoolboys with whom he associated when they discovered where he was being educated. Your British public-school boy (which is the same as an American private-school boy, of course) is very school-conscious and nothing floors him quite so much as a chap coming from some out-of-the-way place that no real public-school chap has ever heard of. After all there are no more than three or four really topnotch public schools in England, and there was one thing Philip's London friends were damn sure of, this place in the North of Scotland was not one of them.

The fact that Philip was a prince would not affect their casual scorn. Public schoolboys are as democratic about titles as they are snobbish about schools and regiments, and they would stand no nonsense from an English prince if he appeared on the scene, let alone a damned Greek.

This must have been quite a tough barrier for Philip to overcome. Neither then nor at any time has Philip been typical of the British aristocracy. But his position in society made him an automatic guest at every junior party thrown in London. He met Elizabeth, now eleven years old, several times during the Coronation, and in Elizabeth's eye the small light of hero worship began to dawn.

Many things happened in the world in 1938, the most important of which was Hitler's seizure of Austria and, later, Munich. Up in Gordonstoun Prince Philip rose to become head of the school, and began to realize that his naval career was almost looking like a national necessity. He was no longer footloose. The Marchioness of Milford Haven looked after him and so did the Mountbattens when Lord Louis was not at sea. Philip had totally forgotten the Greek Orthodox religion and, on Sundays, attended the Anglican services with the other students. He planned ahead to 1939 when he would be in a legal position to take British citizenship. Germany, where under other circumstances he might have grown up, was looming as a hostile power which Philip regarded with the same revulsion that every Briton did. If ever he worried about his sisters—and he was very fond of them in his detached and casual way— he was too proud ever to let it out in conversation. His mother, devastated by the family misfortunes, began to find her only consolation in her religious faith. Some time later she joined the order of Martha and Maria.

In 1939, with his uncle's recommendation, he enrolled at Dartmouth, which is the English equivalent of America's Annapolis. In a confidential report which later became famous, Kurt Hahn, now a naturalized British citizen, wrote to My Lords Commissioners of the Admiralty: "Prince Philip is a born leader, but he will need the exacting demands of a great service to do justice to himself. His best is outstanding. His second best is not good enough."

The words were prophetic. Today they are comforting. When Hahn mentioned "the exacting demands of a great service" which were necessary for Prince Philip to do justice to himself, he was thinking of the Royal Navy. But the words apply even more significantly to the position which Philip occupies at the present time.

He was immediately popular with his fellow cadets at Dartmouth. His sporting prowess was formidable, and there were times when Philip, without realizing it, became a bit of a bully. But that was born of his natural sense of leadership and he soon got over it. In its place came a boisterous taste for practical joking and horseplay which has amused many of his friends and caused him to be cursed to damnation by many others.

He spent his holidays in Europe in those last gay days before the war blacked everything out. In England he learned the glorious education of the English pub and the joys of foaming ale drawn by buxom barmaids.

One thing which constantly irritated him was his title, Prince Philip of Greece. People who asked him for his autograph made him unnecessarily angry, and occasionally bobby-soxers would stare nonplused into their autograph books after Philip had signed himself with a flourish as "The Earl of Baldwin" or "Winston Churchill." Not very funny but it relieved his feelings. When he first joined, the Admiralty ordered that senior officers should address him as "Prince Philip," but it embarrassed both the officers and Philip, and inevitably it was telescoped down simply to "Philip."

He continued to see Elizabeth, and as they grew older the five-year gulf between their ages began to seem less important. When the King and Queen came to Dartmouth to review the Fleet in Weymouth Bay, Philip was invited aboard the Royal Yacht, *Victoria and Albert.* The Commanding Officer had been discreetly reminded that Philip was a relation of the Royal Family so he was also invited when Elizabeth and Margaret came to tea in the officers' mess. Favoritism is never popular but royalty has never found a way of eliminating it except by working extra hard to be a good sport when in the presence of less privileged associates. Philip at the time was a "Captain's Doggie," Dartmouth-ese for a sort of general messenger boy, and rated approximately on par with a Chinese coolie. But however menial the tasks he was doing he was hauled up to keep the princesses company, escorting Elizabeth round the college or playing croquet with her on the lawn, all the time under the envious eyes of other captain's doggies armed with binoculars.

Philip, as usual, overcame his handicaps and his success at Dartmouth was almost, if not quite, meteoric. He won

45

the King's Dirk as the best all-round cadet of his term and the Eardley-Howard-Crocket prize as the best cadet of the year.

He did it just in time to save England. The war began in 1939, and for a few impatient months he carried on with the final stages of his training, and, with the other cadets, chafed frantically at home while the Royal Navy brought the remnants of the British Expeditionary Force back from Dunkirk. Shortly afterward he joined the service proper and, as a midshipman, went aboard HMS *Valiant* to take part in the war against Mussolini in the Mediterranean.

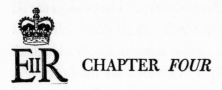 CHAPTER *FOUR*

Until the affair of 1939 to 1945 Royalty was usually cushioned from the full impact of war. In World War I, King George V banned wines from his tables, a gesture which, according to an old clipping at my disposal, proved that "His Majesty was now sharing the hardships of his people."

Later years have seen European and African monarchs abruptly departing their kingdoms, accompanied or followed by wagonloads of family and state silverware. It was all on a somewhat comic-opera level.

But Buckingham Palace was not comic in World War II, and the opera was Wagnerian. The Blitz was a monster of many different aspects to many different people. It killed 29,000 Londoners and injured another 140,000. It obliged thousands to hibernate in the London subways "for the duration." But possibly the majority of Londoners elected to ignore it as best they could and they slept in their beds through the worst of raids.

There was one thing which gave comfort to nearly everybody except those citizens living near the docklands or the Battersea Power Station. London was so vast that one felt protected by one's anonymity. "The chances are on my side," we used to say, which was all very well if one lived in any of London's endless suburbs. But Buckingham Palace was the easiest target in London for the *Luftwaffe*, easier even than St. Paul's Cathedral or the Houses of Parliament. On moonlight nights from the air it gleamed white in a circle of trees and was unmistakably pinpointed at the end of the broad, silver Mall.

It took two direct hits, both when the King and Queen were in residence. A few days after the death of King George VI in February, 1952, Mr. Churchill described to the nation one of the hits in these words:

". . . The King had just returned from Windsor. One side of the courtyard was struck and if the windows out of which he and the Queen had been looking had not been, by the mercy of God, open, they would both have been blinded by the broken glass instead of being only hurled back by the explosion. Amid all that was going on, although I saw the King so often, I never heard of this episode until a long time after. Their Majesties never mentioned it or thought it of more significance than a soldier in their armies would of a shell bursting near him."

Perhaps the most compelling part of this tribute comes in the last two sentences rather than in the exact description of the incident. During the Blitz everyone had his "bomb story." The writer of this book spent most of the Blitz in

London and had half a dozen experiences which he recounts with commendable attention to detail to anybody un-guarded enough to show interest. But he never had as close a shave as this. The wonderful thing about the King and Queen was not their courage in withstanding a near miss, but in the fact that they did not boast about it afterward. They must have been the only people in London with that much self-restraint.

Elizabeth and Margaret were safe at Windsor, but that was little consolation to imaginative girls aged fourteen and ten who knew their father and mother were right in the middle of the firing line.

By now Elizabeth and Philip were close and serious friends. With the concealed British enthusiasm for danger which foreigners always mistake for a stiff upper lip, they both went to war. As has been the case throughout the history of man and woman, Philip's war was exciting, rough, and vigorous, and Elizabeth's was drab and lacking in any sense of inspiration.

Food and clothing ration books made no concessions to a princess. Elizabeth had her one egg a week or gave it to Margaret. She knitted socks for soldiers, worked for the Red Cross, and entertained British and Dominion service-men to tea at Windsor Castle.

She also paid regular visits to wounded soldiers in the hospitals, a particularly horrible function which must have taken all the will power of a young girl sheltered all her life. One Guardsman, severely wounded at Dunkirk, said some years later, "It could have been the most embarrassing moment of my life but it wasn't. I had been hit in the leg and the stomach and was pretty badly shocked. I twitched with nerves every time anybody talked to me. Well, you can imagine when Princess Elizabeth turned up I nearly twitched myself out of bed and on to the floor. But she just chatted at me for a few minutes, didn't ask me any questions, so I wasn't forced to try and talk. I was twitching all right but she didn't seem to notice. Afterward I felt better. I thought I behaved rather well considering the circumstances, and the Princess was marvelous. I wouldn't have liked my own daughter to see me then but Elizabeth didn't turn a hair."

Elizabeth's shortage of clothes was pathetic. Time after time she turned up at public functions wearing the same old austerity uniform of a plain tweed jacket and skirt. At one time the Board of Trade received up to ten letters a week from people asking them to relax the clothes rationing for Princess Elizabeth because people were tired of seeing her in the same old outfit.

The subject actually came up at Buckingham Palace. King George was agreeable but Queen Elizabeth said "No." She didn't think it right in such times for Princess Elizabeth to get such concessions. So the Princess continued to buy clothes at the rate of one new dress a year, augmented by a few hand-me-downs (not always suitable) from her mother.

During the war there were always a few people in London ready to sneer that part the Royal Family were playing "with their blooming bomb-proof shelters." (No such thing, in fact, existed. The shelter at Buckingham Palace would have been atomized by a direct hit and it was never used anyway.) No family had a greater complexity of personal anxieties than the Royal Family, and such was the nature of things that it was Princess Elizabeth who bore the chief brunt of the worry.

The King and Queen were totally immersed in their war work. Princess Margaret was too young to know what was going on. Elizabeth was alone and deserted at a highly impressionable age. She worried about her father and mother in London; from the battlements at Windsor she could see the glow of fires in the London sky. She worried about her uncle, the Duke of Kent, who was serving in the RAF—he was killed in August, 1942. And she worried about Philip, whose current assignment with the Mediterranean Fleet at a time when France had collapsed and Italy had just entered the war, seemed guaranteed to give him the shortest possible life expectancy.

The decisions which the King had to make concerning his family must have seemed futile in the extreme to

Elizabeth. Here was England standing alone and producing a new race of heroes, and Princess Elizabeth had to stand aside impatiently at Windsor while her father decided whether or not she should continue to study the German language. (He finally decided in its favor as it was "the language of Schiller and Goethe, as well as Hitler and Goebbels.")

Nobody now seems to remember or care about the fact that Elizabeth's eighteenth birthday came in 1944 when the war was at its peak and British austerity was at its most barren. Elizabeth probably cares least of all. But at eighteen, in normal times, girls start to think about their coming-out parties and deb balls at the Ritz in London or the Plaza in New York. Princesses come of age at eighteen. Parliament gives them a large chunk of tax-free money. They establish their own households and employ their own ladies-in-waiting. If Elizabeth had been eighteen in 1953 instead of 1944, with all the publicity now falling on the Royal Family, she would have had the time of her life and seen her life story told in every Hearst newspaper and woman's magazine in America.

No such thing could happen in 1944. Elizabeth celebrated her birthday with a small party at the home of Queen Mary—Philip, home on leave, was present—and then enlisted in the ATS, British equivalent of the Wacs. Her own idea was that she should make it a full-time job but this quite obviously could not be done. She was too potentially valuable to the country by her ability to relieve the King and Queen of some of their less important wartime duties. Furthermore the King decided that no job was more important than the training of Elizabeth for the Queenship she would one day inherit. The nation wanted to see as much of the Royal Family as they could. No people— Churchill and perhaps Eisenhower apart—were greater morale-boosters than the King, Queen, and Princesses. When they visited bombed districts of London, even though no advance announcement could be made, the local citizens heard about it, and the ruins sprouted with Union Jacks; faces suddenly became clean even though the water mains were not working, and Cockneys who had just lost everything were able to manage a smile and a forlorn cheer. "Gawd bless 'em," I heard one Cockney woman say on one of these visits. "They've got troubles of their own, pore dears."

Elizabeth was needed for such tasks. But every day for a few hours she went to Wellington Barracks, a few hundred yards from Buckingham Palace, to learn the job of an ATS second subaltern, which is English-ese for a second lieutenant in the women's services. She became a qualified truck driver and mechanic. Her mother, Queen Elizabeth, inspected her detachment once or twice and commented, rather faintly, to a friend, "Lillibet is learning to drive a lorry, but seems to be spending a great deal of her time underneath one."

Elizabeth's most important task in 1944 took her from the trucks to a battleship. On November 30 she had to launch England's biggest battleship, HMS *Vanguard*, 40,000 tons of the most up-to-date fighting gimmicks then conceived. Three years later the same ship was to take her and her parents and sister to South Africa on a state visit. The day was bitterly cold and icy northern winds swept the top-secret port from which the great ship was to be launched (it was Clydebank in Scotland). The officials and the dockyard workers shivered in their threadbare clothes. One official made a chattering comment to Elizabeth on the elements. He had to repeat himself and when he did so Elizabeth started slightly. "I'm so nervous I hadn't even noticed it," she said.

She was handed the bottle for launching—not champagne, because this was war, but South African burgundy. Firmly and without visible trace of the nervousness she was feeling, the young Princess declared, "I name this ship *Vanguard*. God bless her and all who sail in her." For some reason there was a delay in the ship's plunge down into the Clyde. Elizabeth, in horror, muttered to Mr. A. V. Alexander, who was First Lord of the Admiralty at the time, "She isn't moving."

But it was a false alarm. After a momentary pause the *Vanguard* slid slowly down the slipway amid the customary cheers and a hoarse rendition of "Rule Britannia" by a half-frozen brass band. The ship was completed in April, 1946, in good time to be obsolete for World War III.

Apart from this momentous event, only two things broke the wartime grind of existence in 1944 for Elizabeth. The King bought his sports-mad daughter a horse, and Prince Philip came home for the first time in well over a year.

There was no secret in court circles now of Elizabeth's friendship for Philip. They corresponded as regularly as either of them were physically capable of doing—which meant fairly irregularly—and they exchanged photographs. MI5, Britain's equivalent of the FBI, had had a few qualms in the early months of the war about Philip's family connections in Germany, but it did not take much of an investigation to show that Philip was heart and soul in the Royal Navy and in the war on England's side.

Philip was now a man, and a veteran. When he turned up in London in 1944 he was burned to a mahogany color and his hair was bleached the color of straw. He also sported a superb golden beard which startled Elizabeth almost out of recognition. It had been nurtured and trimmed into a fine spade shape at sea, but it did not last long on shore.

55

Elizabeth sternly ordered him to shave it off and Philip shortly afterward appeared sheepishly in public clean-shaven.

By now he had developed a taste for a roughhouse form of practical joking which delighted his more boisterous friends and infuriated nearly everyone else. One night at a London bottle party he tripped one of England's titled ladies three times in a row, until she turned and stormed, "Philip, dammit, stop playing the fool!"

He became notorious for the gentle pleasure he derived out of sticking pins in telephone directories and calling up the unfortunate victim of a ten-million-to-one shot for a nice long chat in the middle of the night.

One night during the vicious little Blitz which the Germans ventured in 1944, Philip was invited to a party in the West End, and the *Luftwaffe* was proving uncomfortably lively company. At about two A.M. one of the male guests volunteered to go out and try to find a taxi for himself and his girl friend.

Charing Cross Road at the time was bright with the reflection of searchlights and German magnesium flares. A fire was raging half a mile away in St. James's Street and artillery shrapnel was falling in a metallic rain in the streets.

After an hour patrolling the deserted streets the young man finally found a taxi and won over the jittery cabbie with promises of a sumptuous reward. Together they returned to the house where the party was still in full swing. As he ran upstairs he passed Philip escorting two girls in wraps.

"And guess what," commented the young man bitterly some months later, "the damned Greek not only stole my taxi for himself and his girl friend, but he took my girl, too."

Inevitably his life with Princess Elizabeth was more decorous than this. He attended Elizabeth's eighteenth birthday party at the home of the aged Queen Mary. Like several other friends of Elizabeth and Margaret he called at Windsor Castle to attend the girls' tea parties and stage shows. Windsor was always a standing invitation to the young men who had been in the Princesses' circle of friends since childhood. The parties often included the Marquis of Milford Haven, his naval uniform graced with the Distinguished Service Cross which he won by his courage and leadership on one of the murderous convoys to Malta. There was the Marquis of Blandford and Lord Edward Montagu, both in the Guards, and the Earl of Dalkeith who was in the Royal Navy.

After tea the young men would gather round the piano while Elizabeth or Margaret played and sang madrigals. "Singing madrigals might not sound like fun," one of the young sailors said recently. "Actually they were a lot of fun, and Elizabeth and Margaret were always a delight.

Particularly Margaret, who in those days looked simply radiant."

In time the war ended, and many months afterward Prince Philip came home. He had fought an impressive war through six years of almost unrelieved danger. His first big battle was the Battle of Matapan in 1941, when the Italian Navy was attacked and almost destroyed at a cost to the Royal Navy of little more than scratches and bruises. The battle more or less immobilized the Italian fleet for the rest of the war. Philip was in charge of searchlight control in the battleship HMS *Valiant* and was mentioned in dispatches for his conduct.

Later he commented on the battle in these words: "It was as near murder as anything can be in wartime. We just smashed the Italian cruisers *Fiume* and *Zara*."

Matapan was only the start. He was transferred to the destroyer HMS *Wallace*, also on Mediterranean Service, and in 1942 got his second gold ring, thus becoming a full lieutenant at the age of twenty-one, a rare achievement in the Royal Navy which does not lose its officers at quite the speed of the Army or the RAF. In 1943 he covered the Canadian Army landings in Sicily and helped artillery-wise in some of the bitter fighting which was required before the island was wrested from the German paratroopers. When Mussolini was knocked out of the war shortly afterward, he

H.M. the Queen.

H.R.H. the Duke of Edinburgh.

© Karsh, Ott

The engagement is announced, summer, 1947. And Elizabeth wears engagement ring for the first time.

First photograph of Prince Charles, one month old.

Anne, one month old, with Mother and big brother, leaves for Balmoral, 1950.

Charles' third birthday, with the late King, Queen Mother, and Anne.

Man of deeds: a "forward-defensive" cricket stroke . . . and of words: Philip talks to reporters.

Fun (off stage) at Clarence House.

Water and a sailor's son: Charles with the Queen Mother, Princess
Margaret, at Balmoral.

Charles on statue of elk. Animals, stone, toy, and live, are his great love.

Square-dancing in Canada. One of the loveliest pictures ever taken of
Elizabeth.

Princess, Wife, Mother, Beauty, Symbol . . . now Queen.

Buckingham Palace Garden Party.

returned home for his brief spell of leave in London, then set out for the Far East. In 1944 he formally renounced any claim he had to the throne of Greece. In India he joined his uncle, Lord Louis Mountbatten.

Mountbatten had been fighting a war of staggering brilliance. For years before the war Mountbatten's life, and that of his wife, seemed to bemused readers of the gossip columns to consist of a ceaseless round of pleasure and luxury. Once the war started, however, Mountbatten broke completely with the gay international set and turned all his formidable energies to the job on hand. He helped to found the Commandos, planned some of their most daring raids on the Continent of Europe. In 1942 he became Chief of Combined Operations, the organization formed to plan the ultimate invasion of Europe. In this way he laid much of the groundwork which was later to ease the task of General Eisenhower.

Near the end of 1942 he was transferred to the Far East where he became Commander of all the British and American forces in that part of Asia. Meanwhile his wife Edwina, always one of the best-dressed women in England, had put away her lovely dresses, and began to look equally chic in uniform. She became a leader in the war work of British women.

It was while Lord Louis was in command in Southeast

Asia preparing for a shock invasion of Jap-held Malaya (an invasion which the Hiroshima bomb made unnecessary) that Philip turned up in the neighborhood. For a while he worked as an aide-de-camp to Lord Louis. Then he went to Australia and fell in love with the place. The raw, tough, earthy Aussies made an instant appeal to Philip, who himself was no "long-hair." He shared such Australian passions as beer-drinking, athletics, and cricket.

He became chummy with an informal, tough, and merry band of Australian acquaintances and, not for the first time or the last, found himself in trouble at court. The Duke of Gloucester, Elizabeth's uncle, was governor-general of Australia at the time and found himself in a brisk political battle with the Australian press over an appointment.

Philip enjoyed the fracas and someone told the Duke that Philip, in arguments, was taking the Australian side against him. According to the reports the Duke hit the roof, and relations between Gloucester and Philip have not been too warm ever since.

The incident was interesting chiefly because it points up, for purposes of comparison, the type of person that Philip chiefly likes to meet, and it certainly reflects no discredit on him. Left alone, King George VI enjoyed his trusted circle of county nobility. The Duke of Windsor and Princess Margaret have always preferred sophisticated café society people. Philip is drawn to the rugged, hearty crowd that likes to drive fast cars as fast as they can be driven, and relishes an occasional booze. Australia represented an ideal way of life for Philip, and it is his favorite country after England. From Australia he joined the destroyer HMS *Whelp* for the final assault on Japan. He was present when General Douglas MacArthur accepted the surrender of the Japanese Fleet in Tokyo Bay, and celebrated VJ night in Tokyo.

Back home in late 1945, he was reunited with Elizabeth and began a courtship which, despite the frequent rumors, was one so discreet and quiet that it defied even the British and American press. Most people guessed at the truth but few people ever learned the details. In fact their efforts to keep out of the public eye became a sort of a game for them. They saw *Oklahoma!* (separately) at Drury Lane and "their song" became "People Will Say We're in Love." For them it had both a lovers' and a humorous attraction, and today it is still one of their favorites.

"Don't throw bouquets at me" (Isabel Bigley and Howard Keel* sang to each other in the London production at Drury Lane). "Don't please my folks too much. Don't laugh at my jokes too much. . . . Don't praise my charms too much. Don't dance all night with me. They'll

---

*Now a Hollywood film star. He was then called Harold Keel and became famous for his London performance as "Curly" in *Oklahoma!*

see it's all right with me. People will say we're in love." * It could have been written for Elizabeth and Philip.

But opportunities to meet could be found, and they were found. Philip had been transferred to a shore naval establishment at Pwlhelli (unpronounceable) in Wales and later to another shore base called HMS *Royal Arthur* at Corsham in Wiltshire, where he gave courses of instruction to petty officers.

Elizabeth and Philip met frequently at Buckingham Palace. If there was a crowd at the front of the building—and there usually is—he would skim round in his fast little MG sports car to the side entrance. They met at Sandringham and Windsor. They met at the Chester Street home of the Mountbattens with the enthusiastic encouragement of Mountbatten himself. They met at Kensington Palace, the home of the old Marchioness of Milford Haven. For this magnificent old woman these meetings must have compensated in full for the tragedy of her early life. She had been married to Prince Louis of Battenberg, Philip's grandfather, a German-born nobleman who was passionately loyal to England. During World War I, anti-German feeling in Britain was so intense that Battenberg was obliged to leave his important position at the Admiralty, even though he had become a British citizen and anglicized his name to Mountbatten. He died shortly after the war was over. Now the Dowager Marchioness saw her grandson moving steadily on the road to marriage with the girl who, one day, would become Queen of England.

Finally, in the fall of 1946—a glorious golden fall that presaged a winter of unprecedented disasters for England—Elizabeth and Philip met at Balmoral, the King's home in Scotland, and on the banks of a loch in the tradition of British Royalty, Elizabeth made her wishes known.

The proposal was merely a formality. They both knew their destinies. They had known it since the early days of the war. Hand in hand they tramped back to the superb castle of Balmoral. By some unaccountable magic there was champagne waiting for them in an ice bucket when they got back and the King and Queen were waiting for them, smiling. What effort those smiles required is a secret that may never seep through the unrevealing silence of British Royalty. They both had come to love Philip but they had had their moments of anxiety. Philip's birth, nationality, upbringing, and parentage were all suspect among the comfortably secure members of the Royal Family, most of whom had a profound distrust of their pauperish foreign relatives from Europe.

More unfortunate than that, however, was the delicate influence of Philip's "Uncle Dickie," Lord Louis Mountbatten. Although the King had to remain above politics, his views were always Conservative, and now Mountbatten was associating intimately with the newly elected Socialist government. Not many months later Mountbatten was appointed Viceroy of India and gave independence to that troubled land; this act stamped Mountbatten in the minds of many of the British aristocracy as a "traitor to his class" and stimulated an unpopularity which, in a milder way, is similar to the unpopularity of the late President Roosevelt among equivalent classes in America.

The partnership of Lord Louis Mountbatten and his wife was a formidable, powerful, and ambitious one. The couple's association with the Labor party and close friendship with the Duke of Windsor were not likely to endear them to the Royal Family, and the Mountbattens certainly felt some chill in the atmosphere at Buckingham Palace. Now, Mountbatten's nephew and protégé was to marry the King's daughter, and not only that but planned to adopt the name of Mountbatten once he became a British citizen.

These were all problems which the King had kicked about in his mind for years. But he was too kind a man and too devoted a father to let them stand in the way of his daughter's happiness. Between King George and Princess Elizabeth was a bond that was unbreakable. The King's marriage to Elizabeth Bowes-Lyon was, in its way, idyllic, and he adored his second daughter Margaret, whose good spirits never failed to elevate and cheer him on the fairly frequent occasions when he felt down in the dumps.

But neither of these relationships ever reached the depth of the subtlety of his relationship with Elizabeth. It was intensified perhaps by the knowledge that one day Elizabeth would take his place on the throne, a thought which must have haunted the King at all times. Many times close observers had watched Elizabeth as the King hesitantly prepared to make a speech. Elizabeth's eyes never left him. At first she would twist the necklace which he had given her pearl by pearl on every birthday since her birth. Then, as he got into his stride and his nervousness disappeared, Elizabeth would visibly relax, too. Because Elizabeth loved Philip, it was an essential part of the King's nature that in time he came to accept him, also. King George, moreover, was a keen judge of character and he quickly saw that Philip, physically, mentally, and by force of character, stood head and shoulders over the rest of the crop of eligible bachelors. Ultimately they became good and trusted friends to each other, though they never came round to having much in common.

The engagement was acknowledged and celebrated over champagne at Balmoral. But in spite of the circumspect nature of their relationship, it was agreed that they would have to tread carefully. Many obstacles and delays stood in the way of their marriage. Philip was still a Greek subject, for one thing. Lord Louis Mountbatten had sponsored his application for citizenship but no strings could be pulled to quicken the citizenship procedures. The British Socialist government was still riding on the crest of national enthusiasm and the British nation, always tensely class-conscious, was particularly touchy at this time about any unnecessary privileges that might be accorded to the unpopular upper classes. Philip would have to wait his turn behind all the other dispossessed Europeans lining up at the right for a blue passport.

For another thing, the Royal visit to South Africa was imminent. Princess Elizabeth was scheduled to spend her twenty-first birthday in the Dominion and address the Commonwealth from there. South Africa, it was felt, was a complicated country anyway, with more collective chips on its shoulder than could easily be counted; and there was no need to confuse its unpredictable outlook on life with a premature announcement of Elizabeth's engagement. Any announcement, then, would have to wait until Princess Elizabeth returned from South Africa, and until Philip obtained his citizenship.

It was a serious young man who left Balmoral to return to his station in Wiltshire. The newspapers learned of the secret engagement with efficient speed, and reported it in detail. They were not a whit put off by the routine denials that emanated from Buckingham Palace. Philip had to put up with some good-natured ribbing from his fellow officers, but generally speaking he was too preoccupied to notice it much.

Philip was nobody's fool, and he knew what he had let himself in for. The job of a husband to a Princess who would one day—perhaps soon—become Queen was a tough assignment for anybody—tougher, perhaps, for a self-made character like Philip than for some of the better-housed and better-titled bachelors among England's noble families.

His situation was too uncomfortably like that of his predecessor and great-grandfather, Prince Albert, Consort to Queen Victoria. Like Albert, Philip was a foreigner. And the British people after two world wars were probably suffering even more from xenophobia now than they were in Prince Albert's time. Albert had been chronically unpopular. Philip enjoyed his popularity among his friends and did not relish the thought of having to take what Albert had taken from hostile British politicians.

Philip had studied history. As soon as Prince Albert came to England, the House of Commons promptly cut a suggested annuity of £50,000 (then $250,000) a year down to £30,000 ($150,000). For the first few years of Victoria's reign, Albert was a cipher, an unwilling buffoon. "Albert helped me with the blotting paper when I signed," the Queen once wrote in her diary. Philip did not fancy spending his life handing Princess Elizabeth her blotting paper. Others might have found compensations in the historic parallel. Albert, in time, grew to be the dominating influence in Victoria's life, and it was his grave, humorless example which inspired the Victorian age. If Philip were to exert a similar influence, the new Elizabethan era might be a very gay one.

But this was looking a long way into the future at best and was, most likely, nothing more than a pipe dream. Gloomily Philip continued to lecture his petty officers at Corsham. "Discipline," he wrote on a blackboard, "is the force which causes a man to play the part required of him in the organization to which he belongs." For many months Philip continued to live his double life and keep to himself the secret of his engagement, a secret, unfortunately, which most of the London newspapers were confidently spreading to millions of readers, including, so it seemed to Philip, most of the personnel of the Royal Navy.

He began to throw himself into cricket, soccer, swimming, and polo as if he were buying time. He drank ale by the pint at the Methuen Arms, his local pub, and competed at darts and skittles (bowling) with the nearby inhabitants. He drove his car very fast, almost recklessly, and tended to lose his temper with taxis and busses in the London traffic jams. He must have known then that his period of freedom was running out and that sometime soon there would be no more beer, no more skittles, and no more spats with competing users of the King's highways.

Elizabeth disappeared to South Africa with her father, mother, and sister in HMS *Vanguard*. She was armed with a battery of photographs of Philip, even including a photograph taken when he wore a beard. Meanwhile, even in the quiet neighborhood of Corsham, Wiltshire, signs of crisis appeared in the nation. Trains were running three and four hours late because of the irregular deliveries of coal. In Sheffield, Yorkshire, 20,000 steel workers, on vital export orders, had six days off while the companies scrounged for coal and coke. Leonard Lord, shaggy boss of the Austin Motor Company, threatened the government that he would close down his Birmingham plant and lay off 16,000 workers unless he got more fuel.

The government had been alarmed for some time, and even Princess Elizabeth was called in to try and stimulate production before she left for South Africa. She attended the Welsh Eisteddfod, traditional Welsh ceremonies dating from Druidical times, and hinted broadly at the miners attending the meetings. "The name of the Welsh miner," she said hopefully, "is the symbol of tenacity and achievement. Never before have so many looked to him for those qualities as today." But down in the pits the miners showed few signs of tenacity and none of achievement, and coal production went down and down.

In January, while the Royal Family lazed away in the *Vanguard* under blue southern skies, and enjoyed the merry hooliganism which sailors traditionally display when they cross the Equator for the first time, the situation in Britain rumbled toward its crisis. With coal stocks at their lowest in the history of the country, the worst winter in living memory buried the British Isles in snow and whipped it with storms. Quite suddenly, in February, the economic structure of the country collapsed.

A desperate government met the emergency with something close to panic. It closed half the nation's industries, including most of the automobile factories, machine shops, and textile mills. Stores, office buildings, and hotels were permitted no power at all for five daylight hours a day. Whole towns were without electricity. The BBC chopped hours off its broadcasting time. Magazines were ordered to suspend two consecutive issues. Newspapers were cut to four pages. Two million people were temporarily laid off work. Cold chilled people out of their morale, courage, and hope. What coal existed was maddeningly out of reach. Colliers loaded with coal were lashed to the piers unable to leave because of the roaring seas. More than 75,000 coal-laden cars were helplessly snowbound.

At Philip's naval base squads of sailors were recruited to dig the establishment out from under the tons of snow, then at night the dark heavens turned white with renewed snow flurries and buried everything once more. Philip lectured the students by candlelight, wearing his naval greatcoat and holding his chalk in blue fingers. In South Africa the King and Queen fretted with frustration at being so far from England in such grim times. Elizabeth stepped up her sporadic correspondence with Philip and kept inquiring anxiously about conditions. Like her father she would have welcomed the chance to return to England and be of some assistance, but there was work for them to do.

Elizabeth, like her secret fiancé, had been somewhat distrait and preoccupied during the voyage from Portsmouth in the *Vanguard*, and left Princess Margaret, bubbling over with excitement, to be company for the both of them. At sea the weather was perfect. *Vanguard* officers invited to the Royal stateroom were impressed, as everyone always is, with Elizabeth's grace, charm, and goodness, but it was Margaret and her performances at the piano which really captivated them. Margaret's gift for mimicry, though less well developed and less stinging than it was later to become, was still remarkable for a girl of sixteen. From mimicry she swung to the classics, then gave a song-and-patter act of her own. She called Elizabeth, protesting, into a duet, finally took it over alone, and crashed into Sousa's "Stars and Stripes Forever" to the words, "So be kind to

our four-footed friends; remember they haven't a mother."
Foolish, but fun. Princess Margaret was an exceptionally
talented girl.

South Africa was Elizabeth's first experience of peoples
over the sea and it was the first time that a reigning sovereign had ever visited the place. The visit was a success,
although the Afrikaans-speaking South Africans were less
demonstrative than the other great dissident Empire group,
the French-Canadians, were to be during the visit of Elizabeth and Philip in 1951. That, undoubtedly, was due to
the greater warmth and ebullience of the French-
Canadians as a race.

Puritanical South Africans were sometimes rather
shocked at the number of times the King and Queen allowed
Princess Margaret to stay up past midnight, but the King
would not alter his habits. He insisted, "This is a family
visit, and Margaret is part of the family." He was com-
forted, as usual, by the careful and loving way in which
Elizabeth watched over her madcap sister. They were in-
separable. The two girls, so different, are so well adjusted
to each other that at no point in their lives have their
personalities conflicted. Their obvious devotion to each
other charmed the South Africans out of their remoteness.

About this time the King noticed that Princess Margaret was using suntan powder and wondered where it
came from, as Margaret had no make-up. Elizabeth was

72

unkind enough to tell. "It belongs to 'Boo' " she said, Boo being Margaret's private maid.

Margaret also raided Boo's lipstick and painted her lips a ghastly orange, a sight which made Elizabeth scream. Then, as sternly as she could for laughing, she ordered her oranged sister to scrub herself clean and shiny.

It was in Capetown that Margaret made her most notable contribution to the *Dictionary of Quotations*. At the Heiress Presumptive's Birthday Ball, Elizabeth, always solicitous for her younger sister, found Margaret sitting out a dance in the marquee. Margaret so seldom sat out anything that Elizabeth inquired after her health and Margaret uttered her now-famous statement, "You look after your Empire and I'll look after myself." The way the remark has been repeated and exaggerated, it sometimes sounds as though Margaret were being petulant. Actually she was enjoying herself immensely and those words told only half the story. What has been lost in the retelling is the fact that both girls immediately burst out laughing and, clasping each other's hands, went back to the ballroom together.

Elizabeth, too, made a much-quoted statement during the South African visit. It was when she was preparing the speech she was to make to the Empire on April 21, her twenty-first birthday. She outlined her ideas and a draft was made for her by the court advisers in the en-

73

tourage. The King's Private Secretary, Sir Alan "Tommy" Lascelles, saw her in the corridor of the White Train near Bloemfontein and asked how the speech was coming along.

"It has made me cry," said Elizabeth.

"That's fine," said Lascelles. "If it makes *you* cry, it will make all the millions of people cry who hear it. That is just what is wanted." Probably fewer tears were shed in the Empire than Lascelles estimated, but even so Princess Elizabeth's speech was an exciting and moving performance. It was spoken with simplicity and caught, for the first time, some of the air of exhilaration and expectancy which Elizabeth has now carried with her to the throne of England. In her speech she pointed out that although she was 6,000 miles from the country of her birth, she was not 6,000 miles from home. Home for her was wherever the 500,-000,000 members of the Commonwealth lived.

"Our difficulties are the great opportunity for you and me," she went on simply. "William Pitt said England had saved herself by her exertions and would save Europe by her example. But in our time we may say that the British Empire saved the world first, and now has to save itself after the battle is won. I think that is an even finer thing than was done in the days of Pitt, and it is for us to see that it is accomplished." Elizabeth then promised to dedicate her life, "whether it be long or short," to the Commonwealth. Monarchs are obliged, by the tightrope on

74

which they perpetually walk, to speak in platitudes, but this was better stuff than most Royal speeches. Millions heard it, and at home, Prince Philip listened with nervousness turning into delight. Afterward Elizabeth appeared with Field Marshal Jan Christian Smuts at a military review which the South African government threw in her honor. She cut a birthday cake at the State ball at Government Hall and danced far beyond midnight.

The Royal Family, in time, returned to their exhausted land. Whatever bromide Elizabeth had delivered to South Africa, Australia, etc., in her birthday speech, "home" was England, and England knew it. Almost symbolically the cold departed and the sun shone and an exuberant crowd of Cockneys cheered the Royal Family home. At Buckingham Palace the Guards, still in wartime khaki, saluted and above the Palace the Royal Standard was run up to the masthead, a symbol of the fact that the King was once more in residence in his capital. Philip's citizenship, which he had been seeking ever since he was eighteen, finally came through; he was now twenty-six. He became plain Lieutenant Mountbatten and threw a noisy celebration party in the West End. His engagement to Princess Elizabeth was announced, after five previous denials, and in July he formally abandoned the Greek Orthodox Church, and joined the Church of England.

With the announcement of the engagement, Philip's

worst apprehensions were immediately realized. The following day he found himself tailed discreetly by a sleek, silent detective. His protests to Scotland Yard were in vain. The detective stuck to him from then on.

Philip now began a strained and unnerving period, and he quickly snapped off any tendencies of his fellow officers to rib him. It might have been acceptable once, but Philip wisely realized that from now on it would be bad form and unfair to Elizabeth. The anxieties told on Philip to such an extent that he piled his MG in a ditch driving from London to Corsham, an unpleasant accident that fortunately left him unscratched. Knowing that he was about to acquire a large sleek Humber shortly, Philip salvaged his beloved little sports car and gave it to Lieutenant Commander "Mike" Parker, an Australian, and his closest friend. Parker is now his private secretary.

On November 19, 1947, the fashionable Dorchester Hotel in Park Lane suffered the bachelor party to end all bachelor parties. It was thrown for Philip by Commander Norfolk, his old commanding officer in HMS *Whelp*. Lord Louis Mountbatten, now dignified with the title of Earl Mountbatten of Burma, just back from the business of unleashing India from the Empire, was among the eleven guests. So was the Marquis of Milford Haven, Philip's cousin and best man. It started rather quietly and ended up in a brawl.

They drank sherry before dinner and champagne with the meal. Unfortunately a few of the guests switched to beer afterward. Near midnight a few press photographers were invited in to take pictures of the guests. "I'm being outflanked," Mountbatten was heard to holler as he saw a photographer move round to get a side shot. A few of the guests cadged flash bulbs from the photographers and hurled them against the walls, uttering bloodcurdling war whoops as they exploded.

Philip left the party at twelve-fifteen, one of the few guests who was still quite steady. Now that he is the Duke of Edinburgh and husband of the Queen, Philip has adopted the oath of silence and the Royal mask of inscrutability so we do not know with what nostalgia he looks back on that party.

It was as much the dividing line in his life as the party on VJ night divided into two the life of Princess Elizabeth. From then on he could go on no more wild sprees, no more of the week ends in Paris that your true Englishman regards as part of his heritage, no more practical jokes. This was the last of his happy life as "just Philip."

A life of dedication had to take its place. How easily would such austerity sit on the shoulders of this informal, smiling Prince? We are still discovering.

 CHAPTER *FIVE*

The wedding of Princess Elizabeth and Prince Philip
was the first great feast of color, light, and brilliance England had seen since King George VI's Coronation in 1937.
It was a movie première, an election, a World Series, and
Guy Fawkes Night all rolled into one. The Household Cavalry were seen, for the first time since before the war, in
their plumes and glistening breastplates. Their horses were
drilled down to the last flank and fetlock, and looked as
proud as if they had never heard that the tank had re-
placed them in modern warfare.

Into London came hordes of the crowned and de-
crowned heads of Europe, eager as always for a big British
Royal ceremony, hovering around their rich cousins in
England for the warmth and security that was as dead in
their native countries as the divine right of kings.

Yet none of this splendor might have happened at all.
Britain was still badly hurt from the dreadful winter of
the year before. Some lightening of morale had been noticed by observers around July and August but, in effect,
the year 1947 touched the utmost depths of Britain's misery.

Today, when the country has painfully but unmistakably found the means for returning to normal, it can throw a Coronation or a Festival of Britain and more or less hang the expense. But in 1947 austerity had become so much the accepted part of British life that even a bouquet for one's girl friend was considered antisocial, and Christian Dior's current New Look was almost heretical.

Nobody felt the cold more than the Royal Family. Pomp was an integral part of royalty's existence, and even in those postwar days it was considered necessary for the King to be seen in uniform and be drawn on various ceremonial occasions in an open coach. But it was fashionable for the King and Queen to be slightly apologetic about such pageantry as they employed, and when the engagement was announced it was put forward as a possibility in some quarters that it should be a quiet affair at St. George's Chapel, Windsor.

There was, admittedly, precedent for the suggestion. The Royal Family right up to World War I considered marriage to be a family affair. Edward VII had been married at Windsor. Queen Victoria and King George V were both married in the Chapel Royal at St. James's Palace. But the newsreel age after World War I changed all that, and the public in subsequent years were dazzled by a succession of flashy royal weddings.

A suggestion that the military escort should wear wartime battle dress was taken quietly at first. Where the protest first began it is impossible now to define; but within a matter of days the populace was shouting in anger, the newspapers were running fulminating editorials, and the Conservative Opposition in the House of Commons was alternately savage and sarcastic at the Labor government. It was a genuine example of spontaneous ferocity on a national scale.

Almost before people realized it, the nation had a half-million-dollar festival on its hands. Supply officers of the Guards found themselves desperately thumbing their prewar ledgers to find out where the scarlet and gold uniforms had been stored since 1939. Norman Hartnell, called in to design a wedding dress, dreamed up a creation in ivory satin inspired by a Botticelli painting. It was so ambitious it took thirty-five experts to put it together.

The former Prince Philip was now plain Philip Mountbatten with a registered address at 16 Chester Street, London S.W. 1., the home of Earl Mountbatten and his wife. The public waited breathlessly to see whether Elizabeth would submit to the pattern of the Socialist-minded times and become plain Mrs. Mountbatten. They found out on the eve of the wedding when Philip knelt before the King. With a naked sword King George touched Philip on each shoulder and turned him into a Knight Companion of the Most Noble Order of the Garter, Duke of Edinburgh,

Baron Greenwich of Greenwich in the County of London, and Earl of Merioneth. These titles were Scottish, English, and Welsh respectively, which, for a young man who six months before had been a Greek, must have set up something of a record.

November 20, 1947, was a day unutterably representative of English Novembers, but nothing could dim the spectacle. The Household Cavalry was breath-taking, and so was the Irish State coach. The bells of London pealed. The crowds cheered and sang. The arrival of the bride and her father at the great West Door of the Abbey was timed with the strains of the National Anthem, "God Save the King," and those observers who recalled Benjamin Franklin's statement about patriotism being the last refuge of scoundrels tried hard not to feel patriotic, but unanimously failed. "Millions will welcome this joyous event as a flash of color on the hard road we have to travel," Winston Churchill had said in the Commons, and his estimate of the figure was, if anything, conservative.

Five kings, eight queens, eight princes, and ten princesses were among the congregation in the Abbey. They included young King Michael, then in his last weeks as monarch of Communist Romania, the Scandinavians, Frederick IX with Queen Ingrid, King Haakon VII of Norway, Crown Prince Gustaf Adolf and Crown Princess Louise of Sweden, Prince George of Denmark (with an eye, they said, on Princess Margaret). There was Philip's mother, Princess Alice of Greece, who now devoted herself entirely to religious work but surprised the other guests on this occasion with her vivacity and charm; Lady Milford Haven, Philip's grandmother (who died in 1950); Peter II of Yugoslavia and his wife, Alexandra; Don Juan, Count of Barcelona and Pretender to the throne of Spain; Juliana and Bernhard of the Netherlands, those faithful friends of England; Prince George of Greece and Queen Frederika of Greece; Queen Victoria of Spain, widow of ex-King Alfonso; Prince and Princess René of Bourbon Parma (he was the brother of ex-Princess Zita of Austria); Prince Michel of Bourbon Parma; Prince John of Luxembourg with his sister, Princess Elizabeth of Luxembourg; the Duchess of Aosta; Princess Eugenie of Greece, and a couple of Queen Victoria's granddaughters, Princesses Marie Louise and Helen Victoria.

A few friends and relatives were not there. Philip's surviving sisters were still in Germany. He corresponded with them in his desultory way, and after the war Prince Berthold's son Max went to Gordonstoun to Kurt Hahn's school, but at the time the war with Germany was too soon over for any easy *rapprochement*. The Duke and Duchess of Windsor were not there. The Duke had been invited but refused because the invitation had not been extended to the Duchess, and remained during the day in his suite high in New York's Waldorf Towers, a place which in this age has become a sort of haven for the discontented mighty of the world.

In the center of all the decorations and uniforms, Philip with his meager lieutenant's rings, seemed slender, strained, and boyish, all attributes which help to explain his huge appeal and popularity in England. Elizabeth was as radiant as a bride could be, in spite of a slight mishap when young Prince Michael of Kent, who was a page, trod on her train. ("Those Kents," hissed a guest, "they just can't keep out of the limelight.")

Dr. Garbett, Archbishop of York, made the address. "Notwithstanding the splendor and national significance of the service in this Abbey," he said, "it is in all essentials exactly the same as it would be for a cottager married in a country church in a remote village. The same vows are taken; the same prayers are offered; the same blessings are given."

So Philip and Elizabeth were joined. Hand in hand they walked back down the aisle. One or two middle-aged ladies momentarily forgot the bride to look sternly at Prince Michael who looked sternly back, but this time his tread was sure. Then the couple were once more out in the cold November day with the streets crammed with ill-fed, ill-clothed, but adoring people. They climbed back into the coach and went to the Palace for the wedding breakfast.

For most young married couples this usually signifies

the first easing of the tension that has kept them at a nervous pitch during the ceremony. Philip and Elizabeth had no such relaxation. They appeared on the balcony of the Palace for the benefit of the thousands of people waiting below in the Mall. But even as the King toasted their health in champagne, they knew they had many more gauntlets of cheering people to run before they could expect to find any sort of privacy.

It proved to be even worse than they thought. They set out for their honeymoon with thousands of sight-seers in hot pursuit. For their honeymoon they had accepted an offer made by the Mountbattens to stay at Broadlands, a large estate in Hampshire near the quaint little town of Romsey. They quickly regretted it. Romsey was jammed solid with people giving the local pubs and fish-and-chip shops a record day's business. Cheers drowned out the brass band as the couple arrived. Not until the gates of Broadlands clanged behind them did Philip and Elizabeth find themselves alone for the first time.

Loyalty is very nice if you can get it, but it was a cold night and it was obvious that Philip and Elizabeth must have wished that the crowds would go on home. What a strange thing a democracy is. In a dictatorship or a police state the police have to force the crowds to assemble to cheer their leaders. In a democracy the police have to make them go away.

Unfortunately the crowds pouring into Romsey by the busload were different from the crowds who cheered the couple in London; and the difference was the difference between the "Loyal Subject" and the "Peeping Tom." The fact that it was Elizabeth and Philip who were secluded behind the noble walls of Broadlands was less important to these people than the fact that they were celebrities. Ingrid Bergman and Roberto Rossellini would have attracted just as big crowds. Rita Hayworth and Ali Khan would probably have attracted even larger ones.

For days after the wedding Romsey was seething. All Saturday night people lined up outside the lovely twelfth-century Romsey Abbey in order to see the couple when they turned up for the morning service next day. During the service the church was crammed. Afterward the crowds followed Elizabeth and Philip back to Broadlands. The police did their best but they could not prevent people leaping walls to try and catch glimpses of the couple as they rode polo ponies or tramped through the bare winter woodlands. One day Elizabeth and Philip went pheasant-hunting. They got a good bag, and Philip with admirable self-control refrained from bringing down a couple of skulking sight-seers who had entered the estate and eluded the royal bodyguards.

An ancient king would have beheaded the lot, but Elizabeth's royal prerogatives did not include anything authorizing her to wreak summary vengeance on any of her father's subjects. The few days over, Philip and Elizabeth, following the path of many a royal prince and princess before them, took the icy, snow-covered roads out of England altogether and into Scotland, where the inhabitants consider themselves a superior and more sophisticated race of people than their southern cousins. It was a good move. The royal couple found peace and quiet at Birkhall, the King's estate near Balmoral.

The weather was cold and raw but the scenery in those parts is almost beyond description, and the solitude was wonderful. Philip drove Elizabeth across the countryside in a land rover, and on Sunday there were no more than thirty people in the little Crathie church when they went to the service.

After the honeymoon, they prepared to return to civilization; Elizabeth to her official functions, Philip to the Admiralty, and both to the task of establishing themselves in a home of their own. The King had given them Clarence House on the Mall, a few hundred yards from the Palace, as a permanent residence. It was a squat, five-floor mansion on which many of the old New York Fifth Avenue mansions had been modeled.

It had been occupied once before by a Duke of Edinburgh, Queen Victoria's second son, and later by the Duke of Connaught. But during the war it had not only been bombed but was taken over by the Red Cross who had knocked it about pretty severely.

On the King's orders the workmen moved in to whip it into shape with central heating and up-to-date plumbing. But it would take a lot of time, labor, and pauses for morning and afternoon tea by the British workmen. In the meantime Elizabeth and Philip rented Windlesham Moor, a rambling manor house in Berkshire.

It was the first real home Philip had ever known and it had a remarkable effect on him. Born a refugee and later a perpetual guest all over Britain and Europe, he had never known anything closer to home than a cabin in one of His Majesty's ships. It is probable that if Philip had ever been to a psychiatrist in his earlier life it might not have been difficult to diagnose a longing for a home which even Philip himself never consciously realized.

Suddenly, at Windlesham, Philip changed. He wandered through the rooms, supervised decorations with naval precision. He called in the manor's handyman and with pride of possession ordered him to erect, on the smoothest strip of turf available, a cricket net, or a netting cage in which cricket players practice batting without having to chase a ball for miles. He gave Elizabeth some batting practice; and when, with a woman's lack of reliability in such matters, she lost interest, he drafted his private detective and chauffeur whose amateurish deliveries Philip, the expert, clouted with good-natured contempt into the net.

Philip became a home-lover and, in time, a family man. It is not hard to see that Philip today with his wife and two children is a different person from the efficient naval officer and grinning off-duty playboy of his pre-marriage days. Philip's love of his home has turned what might have been a killing job of transition into a comparatively easy one.

There is always much embarrassment to be endured in the business of royalty and Elizabeth and Philip were to suffer their share. Embarrassment comes from the blinding glare of publicity which is turned on royalty by the press photographers and gossip columnists. Writers can say what they like and the Royal Family is unable to reply. Princess Margaret has suffered particularly on this account. The silence, of course, puts a particular responsibility on the writer to be extra careful about his facts, and respect the position of royalty. Big Bill Thompson's famous statement that he would punch King George V on the snoot if he ever turned up in Chicago was easy bravery for Thompson, because he knew very well that King George V could not possibly offer to punch him (Thompson) on the snoot if he should ever turn up in London.

Philip and Elizabeth had their first embarrassment at the hands of the British Communists, who of course dislike royalty even more than they dislike most other people. For a couple of years after the war, "squatting" was a widespread practice among homeless families. Abandoned military quarters were invaded and turned into makeshift homes all over the country. The government officially disapproved, but the plight of many British families at the time was so pitiable that it rarely acted to eject them.

But the Communists had bigger ideas. They stepped in with well-organized spectacular coups. They rounded up simple-minded families and planted them in empty luxury apartments that had been vacated by the military. Once there, the families locked themselves in and prepared to withstand a siege. Invariably they were removed after one day or two days or three days of newspaper headlines. The London *Daily Worker* always claimed a great victory when they moved families in, and displayed hideous mental anguish when the police moved them out. In this way the Communist party got the publicity, and the families got the boot and were always left in much worse circumstances at the end of the adventure than they were at the beginning.

Shortly before the royal wedding, the Communists pulled the trick again in houses on the estate at Sunninghill Park which the King had given Elizabeth and Philip, and made loud noises indicative of pain and indignation when they were removed by the police. It was unfair publicity and a dirty trick to play on a royal couple who had problems enough.

Then, after the wedding, Socialist MPs put up their usual chorus of hum's and hah's when the question came up about an allowance for Elizabeth and Philip. They always vote in favor of the sums requested by the government, but they like to make a song about it. In the end Elizabeth and Philip were allowed $200,000 a year, which of course is enough to keep even a princess fairly well heeled even in these days.

To compensate for this kind of embarrassment the Royal Family can always find proof of the terrific loyalty of the people. Defenders of royal tradition—and they can be encountered everywhere in Britain and in most places in the Commonwealth—started a great hubbub when the Church of England inserted the name "Duke of Edinburgh" into the formal prayer for the Royal Family. Purists, purple with passion, wrote to the London *Times* insisting it should be "Philip, Duke of Edinburgh." The ruckus got so bad that Herbert Morrison, loaded with precedents, brought it to the floor of the House of Commons. Morrison, who was Lord President of the Council in the Labor government, pointed out that in the reign of George III, for example, the Duke of Cumberland in the royal prayer was always referred to simply as "the Duke." Tradition satisfied, the imperial blood pressure subsided.

Within a month after the wedding, Elizabeth and Philip were back at work. Elizabeth was the more fortunate of the two. The King remembered his own days at the beginning of his marriage when (as one can see now from old Court Circulars) he and his wife, then the Duchess of York, never stopped traveling on official duties, and married life was not much fun for them. So he ordered that Elizabeth be given plenty of time to get settled into her new way of living. After the wedding Elizabeth was freed from all public engagements until February, 1948, and then her engagements were deliberately kept down. Even so there was still much routine work for her to do.

Philip was immediately immersed in a mass of work. His desk at Buckingham Palace was deep with mail, far more than one person could handle. Lady Mountbatten lent him a stenographer and they got to work. Most of the letters contained messages congratulatory or adulatory, with many requests from teen-agers for photographs or autographs.

The Royal Family, regretfully, have to decline these requests. They are not, after all, film stars, and they have to be cautious about distributing their signatures when the King's signature is the thing that makes the British constitution work. These requests are always answered with polite regrets by a court secretary. Philip's mail also included hundreds of letters from old friends, and buried under the pile he unearthed, to his delight, a formal note from the accounts section of the Royal Navy informing him that he was now eligible for a marriage allowance which lifted his first lieutenant's pay from $33.60 a week to $52.43 a week.

The naval work was fairly easy. His domestic adjustment was less so. But then the first few months of married life are often the most difficult, for princesses, sailors, and everybody else. Philip now found himself involved in a series of bewildering and strange tasks. Although he was working full time at the Admiralty, he volunteered to accompany Elizabeth on some official functions in the evenings and at week ends to get the hang of it. He himself was called on to speak at public banquets. He was elected that year's president of the Marylebone Cricket Club which is the controlling body of Empire cricket. He had a new world of formality and protocol to learn, and took his seat in the House of Lords.

He and Elizabeth, with assistance from Queen Elizabeth, had to supervise the work being done on Clarence House. He had to answer, rather unhappily, a questionnaire, sent by an old American friend who asked these questions:

Do you want to come to America? Replied Philip: "Good idea."

Do you think you will? "No idea."

What color dress do you prefer on Princess Elizabeth? Philip, on safer ground: "I always trust her judgment."

How do you feel about all the publicity you are getting? Philip, gloomily: "It's all right with me so long as it does any good."

Between them, Elizabeth and Philip saw less and less of Windlesham Moor. Instead they had to spend many nights in Lord Athlone's rooms in Kensington Palace in London, Philip every day driving Elizabeth to Buckingham Palace where most of her work still had to be done, then driving alone down the Mall to the Admiralty.

It was very new to him, this life, but he was making out—better probably than he himself imagined. He could have taken it more easily than he did; or, in the cricket term which would come to him more naturally, he could have "played himself in." Instead, he tried to learn the business of royalty all at once. And, above all, there was one problem which Philip had to settle for himself. It was how to make his change in his status gracefully.

All over England and Europe there were characters of variable social standing who at one time or another were on first-name and back-slapping terms with Philip. Nobody wants to be a boor or be considered "upstage," and Philip, like most men with a lot of friends, enjoyed his own popularity. Yet, as Princess Elizabeth's husband, he would now have to keep all his old friends to some extent or another at a distance, and many who had once called him "chum," now had to call him "sir."

The fact that Philip made the change, immediately yet imperceptibly, alienating, so far as I know, none of his friends or acquaintances, is one of the greatest tributes to his personality and sense of personal relations with others. It also spoke well, of course, for the officer-training system of the Royal Navy.

As so often happens in marriage, it was only in gradual stages that Philip learned just how remarkable his wife was. Her devotion to her work was tremendous. Her health and vitality were blooming, and she gave a sense of buoyancy and inspiration to everybody she met. The width of her knowledge was startling. Her skill and sophistication in foreign languages were extraordinary. A passion for the turf, evolved from a lifetime of riding horses, watching horses, and occasionally falling off horses, had made her such an expert on the subject of horses and horse-breeding that today she is one of the world's great authorities on the subject. Her childhood curriculum at Windsor Castle during the war had included an intensive study of the great composers, and Philip, who was more familiar with baseball than Beethoven, was amazed at how much she knew about music.

Philip, thanks to a cosmopolitan life, was politically-minded and Elizabeth could discuss politics with him on his own level. This, though, she found harder to master. In the first months after the wedding Elizabeth began to specialize in advanced politics, learning from the top downward by the practical method of receiving daily copies of Foreign Office confidential dispatches.

Elizabeth's guidance to Philip was wise, but, as usual, it was Earl Mountbatten who gave form and direction to Prince Philip's urge to work for his wife and country.

Mountbatten, at the time, was president of the National Playing Fields Association. He arranged a banquet at the Mansion House—home of the Lord Mayor of London —and handed over to Philip the public task of launching this $1,500,000 enterprise designed to give British kids, then romping on sooty street corners and bomb sites, decent playing fields and sports equipment.

This was a job after Philip's own heart. His own childhood had been spent in a sweat of enthusiasm about sports. Thanks to his own natural health and the kind guidance of Kurt Hahn and others, he had become an outstanding performer at cricket, sprinting, swimming, polo, yachting, water-skiing and, to a lesser extent, soccer; a list which almost beats Jim Thorpe. The thought of small boys deprived of footballs, cricket bats, and soccer fields was intolerable to him.

He spoke and spoke well at public meetings. He lectured schoolteachers, and organized national campaigns.

96

He cornered film stars and sports stars and persuaded them into supporting the great cause. In 1952 he won over Frank Sinatra and Ava Gardner for a one-night appearance in London on behalf of the Association.

It was his control over this organization which really gave Philip the confidence he needed for the job as husband of the future Queen of England. He became a human dynamo at public functions, and exhausted a whole series of worthy officials with his intense determination to learn everything about everything, and on the spot. He became famous, or notorious, for his nonstop cross-examination of everybody he met.

He was impatient with the usual rituals of public function. He was never content to be shown merely what the officials wanted to show him. He preferred to skip the ceremonial teatime and pry all over the factory or museum. He seemed to be constantly up in airplanes or down in coalmines. Officials sometimes wondered despairingly if he would ever leave. More than once, after dark, the Buckingham Palace switchboard would get a phone call from some institution that had been visited that day by Philip, and a strangled voice would croak, "The Duke's still here! He told us to call you so you wouldn't be worried."

There was more than mere curiosity or officiousness about Philip's whirlwind campaign. He realized that behind the formidable armor of Elizabeth's strength, wit, and intellect, there was one serious weakness—her lack of contact with ordinary people. All her life she had been protected from the tough business of making a living in the jungle of modern civilization. From time to time she had tried to overcome this. She had visited wounded soldiers during the war and had served in the ATS. And once she attended a juvenile court in London's slummy East End, listening impassively to a succession of rough and sordid offenses indulged in by some of the great city's Dickensian urchins.

But in the end it was from Philip that she would be able to develop the common touch. Philip knew in his youth what it was to be homeless and alone. He knew, too, that in his present position nothing could be easier than to slide into a lethargy of wealth and protocol and forget his spotty past. But by mixing with as many people as he could, by seeing from as many different angles as possible what made the nation tick, he could make Elizabeth, when the time came, the best-informed monarch in British history. He would be her eyes and ears on the world, and let her know what people were thinking outside the walls of Clarence House and the gates of Buckingham Palace.

Philip quickly revolutionized Royal Family procedure by composing his own speeches, and here again he knew he was making use of a privilege which his wife could not claim. Princess Elizabeth could try to emulate him to some extent, but Royal Family pronouncements are so circumscribed by what they are not allowed to say that it is almost impossible not to fall back on the cliché, the platitude, and the bromide.

Philip had no position in life except as the husband of the heir-apparent. He was freer to speak his mind, and even raise a laugh from time to time. His best-known adventure into the studied understatement at which the British are so brilliant was in answer to an address of welcome in Edinburgh. Philip departed from his prepared speech and rambled skillfully about a wartime visit he had once made to Edinburgh. "A hospitable lord provost (Scottish for mayor) stood us dinner one evening before the night train to London," he said. "We discovered that the train was twenty minutes late. The lord provost offered us one for the road. He rushed round, filled up our glasses, and then we discovered the train was another twenty minutes late. This continued for some time, and we eventually decided the train was six drinks late. Many citizens of Edinburgh were surprised to see the lord provost and myself on such good terms as we made our way to the station."

Philip proved a hit in his new job. But how happy he was it is impossible to say. He was anxious to move into Clarence House and start a permanent home, and he was also anxious to continue with his naval career which was sagging under the weight of all his other engagements.

Instead he went with Elizabeth to Paris, a visit which must have made him realize the worst about his changed position in life. For newlyweds Paris in the spring should be as close to heaven as one can get on earth, particularly for a wife with a husband like Philip whose knowledge of Paris nightlife was extensive and based on personal experience. But the couple made the trip as guests of the French government. Paris for Elizabeth meant a cleaned-up barrier of gendarmes and secret servicemen with gun-pockets bulging and peppermints taking away the smell of garlic. Elizabeth laid a wreath on the tomb of the Unknown Soldier beneath the Arc de Triomphe. They paid a state visit to President Auriol at the Élysée Palace. They ate at the famous Tour d'Argent and went to a night club in the Champs Élysées after the nudes had been discreetly handed out an extra issue of feathers and gold leaf.

It must have been colossally frustrating for Philip, who could have shown Elizabeth Paris in all its glory if they had been left alone. It was not a fault of the French government or of anybody else. The business of royalty has simply grown too sublime for the human touch. Philip's one consolation was in winning $10 at the races at Longchamps—and then he learned next day that some Scots back home, already not too amused by his story of the binge with the lord provost of Edinburgh, were hopping mad over Elizabeth going to watch horse racing on a Sunday.

After six months of marriage, however, Philip was fairly settled in the routine. A good deal of his rather clownish earlier exuberance had gone, but in its place had come a mature charm that had won the nation and the Commonwealth, and devastated the hearts of England's shopgirls. Everywhere he went he was frantically bobby-soxed, and later when he made trips down to Cowdray in Sussex for polo games there were minor riots as the girls tried to get close enough to touch him.

He was now stationed at Greenwich, down the Thames, and was keen to get back to sea, but there was a new reason which kept him close to home. At Buckingham Palace on November 14, 1948, the first son of Elizabeth and Philip was born. He was christened Charles Philip Arthur George, and became the first son born in direct line to the throne since the birth of the present Duke of Windsor in 1894.

 CHAPTER *SIX*

Charles proved to be quite a baby. And some time, many years from now, probably early in the twenty-first century, all other things being equal, England is going to find itself with quite a king.

Fifty-four years of ruinous history had passed for Britain since the last prince in direct succession to the throne had been born. But those had been quiet days when it was not considered necessary to make royalty look as much like a Hollywood movie as it is today. Charles was the first prince born to the magic era of television, Hollywood, and hopped-up press agentry.

All over the world the birth was avidly anticipated, with Buckingham Palace in such a state of excitement one might have thought no royal baby had ever been conceived before. News that a baby was on the way put back many of the most pressing problems of the Royal Family, notably Philip's itch to go back to sea, and attention to the King's health which was beginning to decline alarmingly.

The King was so delighted at the news of his daughter's expected baby that he bestowed on her one of those gifts of grace which only royalty can do. He said that any baby she had, whether boy or girl, would have the style "Royal Highness" and the courtesy title of Prince or Princess. Normally only the King's grandchildren in the male line get the title. The King possibly anticipated that having had two daughters and no sons, and Philip being one son among four daughters, girls would probably run in the family. The fact that Elizabeth dutifully produced a son the first time not only made his preparations groundless but proved, not for the first or last time, that Elizabeth, the Monarchy, and the Almighty often have a happy flair for cooperation.

King George took on himself the first problem—where the baby was to be born. Clarence House was still echoing to the crash of hammers, the scrape of saws, and the hiss of teakettles, and Elizabeth and Philip remained at Windlesham Moor. The idea that a future King of England might be born in a rented house was unthinkable, so Elizabeth was moved to Buckingham Palace, and the home of the King and Queen was made ready for the first royal birth there since Princess Patricia (now Lady Patricia Ramsay) was born to the Duchess of Connaught in 1886.

Next problem was the choice of a nanny for the baby. King George VI had had a retinue of nurses. Queen Elizabeth, his wife, had one, Mrs. Knight ("Alla"), a plump, happy Scotswoman who later became nanny to Elizabeth and Margaret. When King George and Queen Elizabeth left on their state visit to Canada and the United States in 1939, Princess Margaret told her mother, "Don't worry about us. Alla will nurse out mummy until you come back."

Nurse Helen Lightbody was Elizabeth's personal choice, reminding her somewhat of Mrs. Knight. She was a Scotswoman too—an important fact, part of the unshakable aristocratic conviction that only the Scots ever produced good nannies, only the English butlers, only the French maids, and only the Irish gardeners. Nurse Lightbody was a smiling self-assured woman in her middle thirties when Elizabeth first met her. Her basic theories about child-raising were to be kind and to stand no nonsense. In Australia, where she worked, the nickname "No-nonsense" Lightbody stuck. Like most nannies she is given the courtesy title of "Mrs." although she is unmarried.

She was born Helen Lightbody in Edinburgh and went to nearby Jedburgh High School where she had the education which is justifiably the pride of Scotland. One of a large family, she settled down after school to look after her brothers and sisters as well as the children brought in by neighbors. When she was nineteen she applied through an agency for a job as nannie, and was hired by a busy doctor with a large family, her only instructions being, "Keep them oot of my way, girrrl." This she did successfully until she decided on a change of air and came to England.

Again she applied through an agency and was hired by the Duchess of Gloucester as nannie to the two small Gloucesters, William, born in 1941, and Richard, born in 1944. Elizabeth before her marriage often visited York House, the London home of the Gloucesters, and though she never commented, she was obviously impressed at the way the nurse kept the two little boys under control. When the Duke of Gloucester was appointed Governor-General of Australia in 1944, Nurse Lightbody went with the party.

By the time Elizabeth was pregnant, the Gloucesters were back in England. Prince Richard was pushing five, Prince William was nearly seven and Nurse Lightbody was beginning to look around for families with smaller children to care for. Then Elizabeth invited her to join her household. How good a selection Elizabeth made can be seen in the affection which today exists between Charles and Anne and their nannie. The affection was put to the test in 1951, when, with Princess Elizabeth in Malta, Charles came down for a week with tonsilitis. Nurse Lightbody never once left his room.

Many people in Britain and abroad were shocked at the intimate way the newspapers reported the birth, but actually royal births have been something of a public spectacle throughout history, and Elizabeth had, if anything, more privacy than many princesses have had in the past. For centuries in France the public was actually admitted to watch the birth so that everybody could be satisfied that the baby really was the heir to the throne of France, thus preventing intriguers from switching babies.

In Britain, too, there had been a long tradition that the Home Secretary should be present at every royal birth. This dates back to the days when the successor to the Catholic James II was causing a first-rate political crisis. The Protestant Whigs had a dark suspicion that the sonless James was planning to produce some bogus heir to insure the succession of his own line. James later did produce a son, James Edward, and the Whigs alleged that he had been smuggled into St. James's Palace in a warming pan. Since then a State minister has always been present when an heir to the throne was born, although in the past fifty years or so the tradition has usually been satisfied by having the Home Secretary relax as well as he could in the next room.

The King on this occasion decided the whole thing was utter nonsense. Hardly anybody, even in England, uses warming pans any more, and he canceled the tradition, thus earning the warms thanks, at least, of the Home Secretary.

Charles weighed seven pounds six ounces at birth and arrived so quickly that the royal gynecologists, Sir William Gilliatt and Mr. John Peel, had to order an anesthetic. Otherwise all went well. Charles bawled in the approved manner. He was christened by the Archbishop of Canterbury. He was vaccinated, inoculated against diphtheria, and circumcised.

The name of Charles was decided by Elizabeth and Philip between them and showed the strong strain of Scottish romanticism which Elizabeth has. For generations after the House of Hanover came to power in Britain in 1714, the name of Charles frightened them even more witless than nature had already made them. They had good reason to worry. The name of Charles was vividly associated with the Stuart uprisings in Scotland in 1715 and 1745.

When the name was announced, every hack journalist, copy-reader, and rewrite man in the English-speaking world christened him "Bonny Prince Charlie." The nickname persisted for a few months then expired. It was positively barred in Elizabeth's household, and it is never heard today. Charles is simply "Charles."

"Angelic" was the first description ever given of Charles, by Countess Glanville, Elizabeth's aunt. But the adjective did not stick very long. Sir William Gilliatt later called him "matey and fearless" which was probably more accurate. Charles was actually a living example of the fact that very small children can be gentle, kind, polite, angelic, and little devils all at the same time.

It was Charles' unshakable *sang-froid* and receptiveness to ideas which endeared him to everybody. A few months after the death of King George a visitor to Buckingham Palace was halted, as so many visitors are, by the small boy who looks even smaller in the huge rooms and endless corridors. Boldly the little fellow demanded where the visitor was going.

"I'm going to see the Queen," was the reply.

"Who's she?" asked Charles.

"Your mother, Charles."

"*Is* she?" said Charles, deeply impressed, and walked away, hands behind his back, mulling over this absorbing piece of intelligence.

Once Prince Philip was on his way back from Malta, where he was stationed, and Elizabeth, with some misgivings, took Charles with her to the airport to greet him. She was rather anxious lest the roar of the engines should be overpowering to small ears. But Charles was not disconcerted in the least. He jumped up and down as the plane landed and was the first to rush forward to greet his father. As if to prove his sophistication beyond all doubt, Charles, homeward bound on his father's knee, was seen to breathe heavily on the windowpane and draw things like cows on the clouded glass with his finger.

Charles has never been allowed to get the impression that he is apart from or better than his fellows, and only in recent months has it been slowly dawning on him that he is something called a "Prince." But long before that he realized that in any show he always has a prominent place. A year or so before the death of the King, when he was not quite three, he was taken to a military ceremony and to his outraged astonishment he was left in his baby carriage. People near the saluting stand heard an indignant little voice saying again and again, "Why can't I stand on the steps with Granny?" Eventually he was allowed to stand between the King and Queen, and was immediately at home, saluting seriously and clapping his hands in time to the massed bands.

The eleven months that separated Elizabeth's wedding and Charles' birth found the economic situation in Britain improving. It was not visible on the surface. Rationing was as severe and the nation was still to buffet its way from crisis to crisis; but underneath, Britain's hidden wells of moral and physical strength were being replenished. It was symbolic of the gradual return to national confidence that on October 26, 1948, for the first time since before the war, the King wore his crown and royal robes at the ceremonial opening of the new session of Parliament. There he made the King's Speech which is more or less the equivalent of the President's State of the Union speech, and it is always a landmark in British pageantry.

It was the last high moment in the public life of King George VI. He was a shy, nervous, and irritable man, but in his worried, harassed way he glowed with a goodness which could never be hidden from the people. Above all he loved his family and 1948 was the twenty-fifth anniversary of his marriage, the twelfth year of his reign, and the year his grandson was born.

Not until a week after the birth of Prince Charles did he allow the world to know the pain he was suffering. An artery carrying the blood to his right leg was on the point of collapse, carrying the danger that the leg itself might wither. The official bulletin referred to a "risk to the limb" which presented to the appalled British people a nightmare prospect of amputation. The official tour which he planned to make of Australia and New Zealand in 1949 was abandoned.

On March 12, 1949, seven of the country's greatest doctors, led by Mr. John Learmonth, a Scottish specialist, operated on the King and saved his leg, and slowly he started to convalesce.

Existence for Philip and Elizabeth in the months following Charles' birth were probably the most wretched in their married life. The King's illness oppressed them with the most awful anxiety. They still had no home of their own but rotated aimlessly from Windlesham Moor to Kensington Palace to Buckingham Palace. The costs of the repairs to Clarence House were spiraling higher and higher, and nothing upsets the Royal Family more than having to call in the House of Commons on unscheduled financial matters.

Finally in January, 1949, Elizabeth came down with measles at Sandringham, an absurd and undignified illness for the normally healthy Princess. As a result the breast-feeding of Charles had to stop and he was fed by a formula.

As usual in times of crisis Philip worked like a horse. He philosophically postponed his return to sea to a still more obscure date in the future and, with the Duke of Gloucester, pinch-hit vigorously at all the official functions which his father-in-law was not able to perform.

The clouds began to lift in May when Clarence House was completed, and the royal couple hustled into it so precipitately that they were in occupation the same day the last workman moved out. Originally the House of Commons had allotted $180,000 for the renovation of Clarence House, but the Labor government later had to ask for an extra $20,000.

It was a home worth waiting for. It had a refrigerator capable of making twenty pounds of ice. Philip, taking one or two ideas from the Mountbattens' gadget-studded penthouse, had a closet which automatically ejected any suit or uniform he wanted by pressing an electric button. The reception rooms were in satinwood, one room being kept exactly as it was when John Nash designed the house in

1825. Everywhere there was antique furniture, Adam mirrors, and George III bracket lights. Philip's and Elizabeth's bedroom suites had connecting doors. Elizabeth's bedroom was designed with soft peach draperies, tinted sheets and blankets, and heavy satin hangings in red rose and cream. On the dressing table she kept the $4,000 dressing table set which had been given her as a wedding present by the Diplomatic Corps.

Philip chose Regency style for his own bedroom though a Regent would have blanched at the modern divan bed he selected for himself. More appropriately, his dressing room was designed like a naval officer's cabin. Elizabeth's bathroom was tiled in cream and white, Philip's in mirrored green. Finally young Charles had a four-room suite of his own with a day nursery in primrose and yellow and a night nursery in light blue and white.

In October, 1949, Philip flew to Malta to become First Lieutenant in the destroyer HMS *Chequers* and began a long and difficult spell of overseas duty, the difficulties being social and domestic rather than strictly naval.

Malta is a delicate assignment for anybody prominent in British society and, of course, nobody was more prominent in British society than the Duke of Edinburgh. It is easier from a sociological standpoint today to write about what is wrong with Malta than with what is right. But first and above all must be remembered the fact of its superb war record. The island took such a beating from the *Luft-waffe* during the war that the King, in an unprecedented and inspired move, decorated the entire island with the George Cross, civilian equivalent of the Victoria Cross. In those days many of its population lived in caves and shelters. The RAF's protective umbrella was tiny but supremely gallant; Buzz Buerling, the Canadian air ace, winning every decoration short of the V.C. for his work in the island's defense. So long as it had only the Italian air force to reckon with, the RAF, outnumbered though it was, could cope with the job. When the Germans came in to reinforce the attack, the RAF was frequently overwhelmed; and convoys from Gibraltar could only break through to the island with supplies at the risk of terrible losses.

By 1949 the scars had largely been covered and Malta had once more become to the Royal Navy rather what Hawaii is to the United States Navy. As an overseas base it has many physical attractions for officers and men stationed there. The sun is glorious, the swimming superb, and the little Maltese towns and villages quaint and exciting. It has a thriving and exclusive British high society. And like all places far from home where there is a powerful, introverted "smart set" it is easy to make social mistakes there. From the start the Duke of Edinburgh was the center of the spotlight and the glittering prize for every hostess. Philip knew he was walking a tightrope and was determined to edge forward carefully.

Meanwhile Elizabeth, left behind in England, uncomplainingly shouldered an enormous amount of work. She spoke to a Mothers' Union meeting about the evils of divorce, unveiled a tablet marking the rebuilding of a blitzed church in Plymouth, laid a wreath at the Cenotaph in Whitehall, attended a war memorial meeting at the Albert Hall, inspected the Grenadier Guards (rather coldly; only a couple of months before she had criticized them roundly in a letter for their noise and bad manners in her presence at the annual dinner) and visited the potteries in Staffordshire, risking her health in a Midlands downpour.

In between times she managed to fly to Malta for periodical visits to her husband, and this became the pattern of the next two years during which time she saw Philip for only eight months.

To Elizabeth, duty was second nature and involved no hardship. She was consequently flabbergasted when one of the London newspapers opened up on her during one of her trips to Malta and suggested sneeringly she ought to spend more time at home with her son. Elizabeth ought to have become thick-skinned by then after newspaper criticisms which had ranged from her hats to her waistline, but this touched a particularly sensitive spot. As usual she could make no reply, but some day the camel's back will break and she or Philip or Princess Margaret will forget the royal tradition of silence and reply to the press and the magazines. It should make the best reading in years.

Elizabeth was thrilled for Philip's sake when, in 1950, he was given his first command, HMS *Magpie*, an anti-aircraft frigate. He also won the extra half-ring on his sleeve as a lieutenant commander, which, after eight years as a humble lieutenant, was the climax to his active naval career. The *Magpie*—*Maggers* to the crewmen—was a tiny ship but a disproportionately large load of responsibility. It does not take long for people to discover whether a man is a good captain or a bad captain. Philip could not afford to be inefficient. From the start expert, hypercritical eyes were on him whenever he ordered a change of course or rang the ship's telegraph. From the shore the sea-wise British and Maltese populations would gather to watch as he entered Sliema Creek.

Philip understood the problem. His first move was to win the crew who were likely to face many wisecracks ashore from other sailors, not to mention the Royal Marines. With that enviable flair for the disarming statement, he called the ship's crew together and told them he realized it might be a source of embarrassment to have the Duke of Edinburgh in command. "But any man who comes up before me on a charge with two black eyes can be sure I will be on his side," he said grinning.

He set to work. On maneuvers in the Mediterranean —and don't think the Med is always sunny and blue; it is often cold and wild—Philip would be up all night, occasionally taking a nap in the chartroom chair. On the bridge he would be wrapped up in sweaters and a duffel coat, warming his insides with hot cocoa brought from the galley, stamping circulation into his feet. On shore he had to look after the ship's business and with his first lieutenant log fractious sailors up before him on offenses.

Malta watched him breathlessly. When Elizabeth flew over, the royal couple lived as quietly and as informally as they could. They rented an old house, the Villa Guardamanja, drove around the island, or strolled openly in the sun-drenched Carmenesque town of Valletta. Elizabeth, eager as always to fulfill her royal obligations, managed to attend public functions and ceremonies every day while Philip was busy on board ship.

Often she would visit the tiny steel wardroom shared by Philip's six officers. Conversation was general, cheerful, and free, with Elizabeth adroitly keeping the subject away from anything that could be construed as taking a liberty with her position. Shortly before one of Elizabeth's visits to Malta, Scottish pranksters stole the ceremonial Stone of

Scone from Westminster Abbey where it had been kept ever since one of the historic Scottish defeats by the English. The ship's officers, Philip included, thought the whole thing was a terrific laugh and said so.

"Do you?" said the Princess disapprovingly. "Well, *I* don't think it's funny at all."

"Change the subject, old boy," one of the officers hissed out of the side of his mouth to another.

For a Princess, Elizabeth's private household was surprisingly small and showed how much she felt her visits to be a release from the usual trappings of royalty. She had three ladies-in-waiting, whose job was to coordinate and help organize all the requests for public appearances which Elizabeth received. There was also a secretary and a maid. Philip was content with a valet. Security arrangements were kept to a minimum, the local police force being simply stiffened by Elizabeth's private detective, a great favorite with the *Magpie* officers.

By 1951 she and Philip had become almost part of the Malta scenery. While the *Maggers* was in port Philip slept at the villa, rising at six-thirty for a quick breakfast. Then he would row himself across the creek in a little boat hired for $2 a week. He would return in the afternoon in time to drive Elizabeth out to a polo game at the Marsa Club.

Once she was a spectator when Philip was thrown

from his pony. Elizabeth, who has fallen off a horse with aplomb more than once, just managed to stifle an unprincesslike cry. But Philip scrambled to his feet, grinned at her reassuringly, and went on with the game.

Philip's job was comparatively easy while Elizabeth was with him. When she was away it became intensely difficult. The Royal Navy has always been a snobbish service, and no matter how efficiently Philip handled his little ship, he still had to try and avoid having the *Magpie* slightingly labeled "The Duke of Edinburgh's private yacht."

At sea he felt more at home. He was a good captain. His crew were reserved but secretly rather proud of him. His relationship with his officers was good. But as soon as the ship was tied up there would be a huge Rolls Royce waiting on the dock ready to drive him to Government House. Ashore he took precedence over the mighty Commander-in-Chief, Mediterranean Fleet. However much it delighted the men, the officers not unnaturally felt ill at ease with a commanding officer who was at one moment almost a brother and at another almost godlike in his remoteness.

Nothing could be done about it. It was just one of those things, but it worried Philip. In an effort to bridge the gap with his officers he went on one or two inoffensive but gay parties, which were eagerly seized on by the Malta gossips and relayed with more and more details back to

London. As a result Philip, on one of his trips home, was given a severe dressing-down from King George.

Philip loved the *Magpie*. In future years he knew he would look back on it as his last few months at the career he planned for himself. It was part of the stuff of royalty that as the years passed he would glitter with new orders and decorations. He would become an admiral, get his RAF wings, and appear in every uniform the English services could devise. Those were formalities. What really mattered was that he had *earned* his two and a half gold rings and his command. Very soon, he knew, he would be recalled from the *Magpie* to what royalty refers to as "higher service," but which Philip is reported to have described irreverently as "bazaar opening."

The call came in July, 1951, after he had captained the *Magpie* for a year. It was a far from jolly sailor who said good-by to his men in the approved naval manner. His period in command, he told them with the sincerity that is one of the great sources of his strength, was the happiest time he had ever known in his naval life.

The sailors listened stonily. It is unlikely that they understood the gloom or the pull of destiny which Philip felt as he made what was in effect his farewell speech to his own naval career.

But in his briefcase as he flew back to London and "higher service" was the text of a speech which was going to rocket him before long into the lead as a molder of affairs. Some months earlier he had been invited to speak in Edinburgh to the British Association for the Advancement of Science. He chose a theme which sounded as dry as dust, called "The British Contribution to Science and Technology in the Past Hundred Years." For months he slogged away at the speech in his cabin, strewing the place with so many notes and textbooks and reference books that his steward raged at the sight whenever Philip was out of hearing.

A few scientist friends had looked over his drafts just to make sure he had made no technical boners, but otherwise it was all Philip's own work, and it took the assembly of leaders in British science by surprise.

Philip described himself as "an outsider, a layman." He had eliminated the clichés from his drafts and launched unhesitatingly into a biting attack on the failure of British industry to keep up with the progress of the rest of the world.

Between 1870 and 1890 Britain became overconfident of its supremacy in the world of industry, he declared. From then on British industry made inadequate use of science.

"Our physical resources have dwindled," he said, "but the intellectual capacity of our scientists and engineers is as great as ever and it is upon their ingenuity that our future depends. . . . The instrument of scientific knowledge in our hands is growing more powerful every day. Indeed it has reached a point when we can either set the world free from drudgery, fear, hunger and pestilence or obliterate life itself. It is clearly our duty as citizens to see that science is used for the benefit of mankind. For what use is science if man does not survive."

It was a good literate speech. The scientists loved it, so did the newspapers, and the delighted British people read it through with a sort of "that's-my-boy" kind of pride.

Philip was elated at the reception. After nearly four years of being married to a girl who was more important than he could ever be, he had found what he was seeking. He could, with care, become the stimulant, the conscience, and, where necessary, the irritant which Britain needed. He was encouraged to keep it up and has done so ever since. He landed a haymaker on the various organizations devoted to road safety, complaining they were "too compartmentalized," and should think of the whole problem not just the problem as it affected them.

He went all-out on plans to further one of the causes dearest to his heart, namely the establishment of closer links between royalty and the Commonwealth, this probably inspired by his personal love of Australia. He was full of ideas, which he was now about to tackle more confidently. Earlier he had not been too successful. He had in

Red roses for the Queen. Visiting a children's hospital in London.

Keystone Pictures,

Trooping of the Color.

Trooping of the Color. Farewell wave.

A new look at the world. Charles is four today.

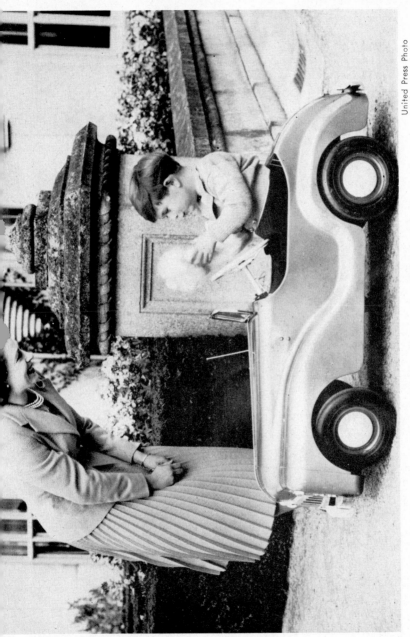

Two presents: a car and a glove puppet.

United Press Photo

Balmoral: holiday retreat of the Royal Family.

Easy for Anne to laugh. But Charles has an Empire to think about.

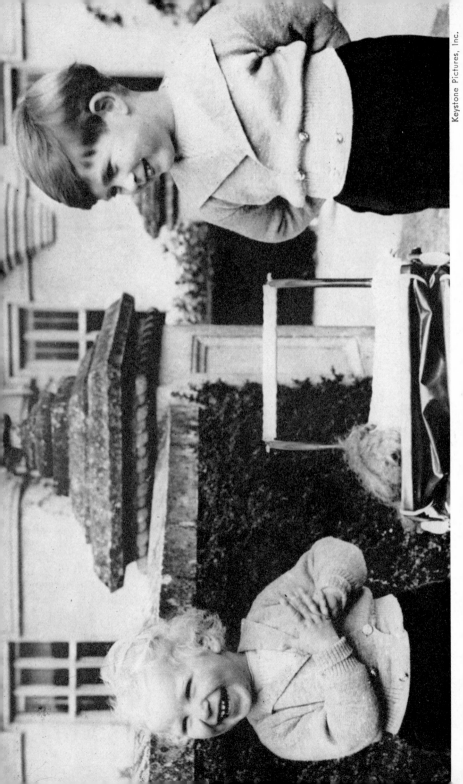

The glamorous Queen attends the Royal Film Performance.

Family picture broken up . . .

. . . by small girl in search of . . .

Critical observer looks on . . . .

...and in time is very new

The best-loved couple in the world . . .

. . . and the most regal.

one speech dreamed up the title of "Metropolitan Dominion" as a substitute for the old, imperial "Mother Country," and dropped it hopefully into several speeches, but it failed to take hold, possibly because it sounded too much like a Parisian subway station.

The Edinburgh speech was a triumphant prelude to the tough months that lay ahead. Before Elizabeth and Philip was their greatest test yet, their forthcoming tour of Canada and the United States, and after that—they assumed—the Australian tour which the King had been obliged to postpone three years earlier.

If they could overcome those two hurdles successfully, the young couple would be ready for anything that might happen to the Monarchy and the Empire. But they did not realize that events were going to happen so cataclysmically and so fast.

CHAPTER *SEVEN*

It is easy to sneer at the problems of royalty. It is understandable for a young wife living in Brooklyn, New York, or Wandsworth, London, harassed by housing shortages, rising food prices, and children which she has to care for from morning to night, to sound off satirically about the "troubles" of a couple living rent-free in a mansion with more than $200,000 a year, a retinue of servants and a "Court" of their own.

It has been one of the favorite sources of crocodile tears to the British Communist party for years.

But Elizabeth and Philip have had troubles all of their own, which the Communists would never acknowledge but which most other people have seen and appreciated. The chief difficulties of a royal marriage stem from the goldfish-bowl nature of their lives and the utter lack of privacy. The newspapers follow every move they make and anticipate quite a few they don't make. They must never show human frailty or weakness. Kings, queens, and princes have to smile and keep on smiling if their feet hurt, if a platform gives way under them, if dissident minorities shower them with leaflets, whether or not they had a reasonable night's sleep the night before, and through a hang-over (not an unheard-of occurrence in the Royal Family, though it has never affected Elizabeth who neither drinks nor smokes). Even the President of the United States can look bad-tempered, shout, whistle, or mug at the camera from time to time. But royalty is allowed only to be gracious. If Elizabeth and Philip and the Queen Mother and Princess Margaret have problems of their own, they have to take good care not to show it in their faces any time when the photographers are around, which is most of the time.

Once when Margaret, in Paris, scowled at photographers who were almost blinding her with flashes, the picture was printed in the more sensational London newspapers with irate comments on French bad manners, and the scowl almost became a political issue.

The Royal Family has borne up well under the weight of newspaper gossip and campaigns. They realize that it is stimulated by the intense interest and affection which is felt for them all over the world, and whatever embarrassment they feel at the more sensational "disclosures" that appear in the magazines, they cover with the strong sense of humor that runs in the family.

One day the King, whose own sense of humor was much more highly developed than he has been given credit for, accosted one of Margaret's boy friends at Buckingham

Palace and said with frowning brows over twinkling eyes, "Young man, I understand from *Time* magazine that you wish to marry my daughter." Another time the assembled family, watching the blissfully innocent Princess Anne at play on the floor, guessed which other noble-born babies would be "linked" to her by the newspapers not many years from now. (The list included Lord Hay, then aged four, Viscount Borodale, aged five; Viscount Gough of Inshes, an old man of ten; and Viscount Ipswich, aged two.)

As Elizabeth and Philip prepared to set out on their Canadian and United States tour in the fall of 1951, they could look back on three years of a marriage that had been dogged at every point with difficulties and pitfalls, yet they could feel they were making a success of it. Mental adjustments had been difficult for both, particularly for Philip. The period following Charles' birth had been particularly trying, chiefly because they did not have a home of their own, and partly because of Elizabeth's illness. Malta had not been an unqualified success. Philip's smile in those days had an unmistakably glassy quality.

But in 1951, despite the troubles that had gone before, it was easy for the public to see that Elizabeth and Philip were a couple who were not only in love but had found happiness.

Court advisers agreed that whenever Philip came into the room Elizabeth's eyes lit up in delight. And if Philip kicked sometimes against the hothouse atmosphere of the court and pined for a return to the Royal Navy and pub-haunting evenings with beer and barmaids, he was more than recompensed with a contented and rewarding family life, something he had never known before.

In August, 1950, Princess Anne was born and turned quickly into a gay, laughing child who adored her brother and after a slow start kept up with him in every stage of progress. The late summer of 1951 marked Philip's return to Clarence House and his oratorical triumphs. A study of the family at this time shows a charming picture of friendship and affection, and is worth deeper examination. Philip's relations with his mother-in-law and father-in-law were excellent. The friendship between King George and Philip was dignified by an immense mutual respect. Everybody who met the King loved him, and Philip with his easy sailor's ways was a great stimulant to him and helped him emerge from his normal tendency toward moroseness.

Philip got on pleasantly with Queen Elizabeth, now the Queen Mother, and with Queen Mary who had been one of the first to see possibilities in the idea of Philip as a future husband for her granddaughter.

Philip and Princess Margaret were firm friends. They had a great deal in common, including a working knowledge of night clubs and small-hour parties. Philip, as a

husband and a family man, had grown out of the adoles-
cent passion for parties, but 1951 was Margaret's great
year. She was twenty-one and had built around her the
famous Margaret Set, consisting of a dozen young upper-
class English men and women and one American girl,
Sharman Douglas, daughter of the then U.S. ambassador.
Their ages ranged from twenty to thirty-one. Their tastes
were concentrated upon dancing, the theater, the arts, and
themselves. To some ambitious debutantes the Set was
the ultimate social goal and ambition; to others, outside,
and a few inside, the Set was a stupefyingly uninteresting
school of scandal and small talk. It began to form in 1948
and continued with only rare changes in personnel until
it disbanded with the death of the King, never to be revived.

Margaret ruled the Set with an iron hand, but some
of her friendships, notably her widely publicized alliance
with vivacious Sharman Douglas, ended rather unhappily.
Sharman returned to the United States with her father Mr.
Lewis Douglas, after his term as ambassador to the Court
of St. James. But her heart was in London's night life,
and she took the first chance she could to return, the chance
being a publicity job with an English movie company. She
then found that a press agent was something different from
the daughter of an American ambassador. No longer was

Buckingham Palace her second home, and after a few months she returned forlornly home to the United States without renewing her friendship with Margaret.

It was not really Margaret's fault. It simply stemmed from the impossibility of a commoner or even a nobleman to find a common level of conversation with a girl in Margaret's position. Etiquette, for example, controlled a long list of subjects that were taboo among Margaret's escorts in her presence. Money was one of them; one could talk about horse racing, but not how much was won or lost. The reason for this is that throughout her life Margaret has never had any use for money. Even tips to powder-room attendants are managed by her lady-in-waiting. Politics were also out. As a member of the Royal Family Margaret had to be above and apart from politics. Margaret's friends usually found it safest—and, let's face it, more enjoyable —to talk about themselves and their friends. It was this atmosphere of gossip and more than a little backbiting that several young men found most insufferable, and departed the Set abruptly.

And even those who stayed sooner or later became engaged and were married. The Marquess of Blandford, the Earl of Dalkeith, Lord Ogilvy, and several others, all childhood friends of the Princess, dispersed into matrimony. Her "steady" boy friend, Billy Wallace, English stepson of Herbert Agar, the American writer and diplomat, drifted away and later described himself as "on the shelf." Few new friends moved in to take their place. Margaret was paying the price for keeping her circle of friends too exclusive for too long.

Whatever the state of Margaret's current love life, however, she always had a sympathetic and loving friend in Elizabeth. Ever since August 21, 1930, when bonfires lit the hills around Glamis Castle to celebrate the first birth of a royal princess in Scotland in over 300 years, Elizabeth had been Margaret's little mother. As a child Elizabeth would not sit down until she knew Margaret had a comfortable cushion to sit on. Elizabeth gave Margaret her toys and took care of her sister with a devotion which Margaret has never failed to reciprocate.

Britain, without understanding the facts about Margaret's private problems, was still proud of the glamorous Princess. Nearly everything she did could be guaranteed to arouse some protest from some organization or other, but the public loved her dresses, her boy friends, and her smoking in public through cigarette holders.

King George, Queen Elizabeth, and Princess Elizabeth were all tolerant of their favorite's unconventionality and her stubborn Hanoverian determination to live her own life as she wanted. None of the Royal Family ever paid much attention to Margaret's critics. They understood what she wanted to do and could remember the bleak nagging wartime years at Windsor Castle when Elizabeth and Margaret were virtually imprisoned for safety's sake, years which carried Margaret from the age of ten to the age of fifteen.

Even now, when she is Queen, with a never-ending schedule of duties, Elizabeth calls Margaret at least once every day and usually more frequently. But it is Philip who really understands Margaret and speaks her language. And Margaret who enjoys lording it over her friends has never been able to get anywhere in this direction with Philip.

"Nonsense," he told her once during a visit when she called to demand breakfast in bed. "It's waiting for you in the breakfast room. Get up and get it."

During the whole period when the Set was expanding and contracting, with Margaret apparently out to night clubs and theaters every night and with a neckline that plunged or rose according to whatever furor had greeted the previous one, Philip stood aside and watched as an amused and understanding spectator.

He sided enthusiastically with Margaret when she fought her battle with her mother for strapless evening gowns. For a long time the Queen put her foot down, but Margaret finally had her way and appeared in a gown that was both a sensational and an unqualified success.

In the emotional history of the British Royal Family,

gravity has always gone hand in hand with wildness, and Philip and Margaret are on the same team. The tradition started when the girl Queen Victoria, a lively, effervescent little creature who used to love dancing until dawn, married the unsmiling Albert. Their pleasure-loving son Edward VII, produced the straight-laced, old-fashioned King George V who had two wild sons, Edward, now the Duke of Windsor, and George, the Duke of Kent, who was killed during the war.

The pattern is still consistent today. King George VI, a grave man, married the cheerful and irrepressible Elizabeth Bowes-Lyon, and the quiet, serious Princess Elizabeth fell in love with the carefree Philip. It is to the far-wild side of the family that Margaret belongs, and her relatives do not begrudge her her fun.

It is a happy party when Margaret joins a family session with Elizabeth, Philip, Charles, and Anne. Margaret is wonderful with children, knows how to amuse them, and has a flair for buying them small, inexpensive gifts which just ring the bell.

As Charles learned to form words, Margaret put her foot down firmly on any idea that he might call her "Aunt." So Margaret to Charles became "Margot." And the rest of Charles' family became "Mama" and "Papa," after the fashion of royalty; his grandmother was "Granny" and his great-grandmother "Gan-Gan," a word born in Victoria's last few years when she was dandling her own great-grand-children—the Duke of Windsor and the late King included —on her knee.

Philip delighted in his family relationships. He was an outstanding father from the start, and it will not be many years from now before he is able to work on his ambition to turn Charles into an outstanding athlete by teaching him to swim, sail, ride, and wield a cricket bat.

Charles' development in his first two and a half years was great compensation for the troubles his parents were having to face. Charles was twenty months old when Anne arrived. The way he was trained to meet her, accept her, and love her showed remarkable astuteness and psychological wisdom on Elizabeth's part. She gave orders first that no one was to tell him that another baby was on the way, feeling that a boy as young as Charles would not be able to understand anything so involved as the arrival of a new sister or brother. Babies of twenty months or even more think only in the present and cannot absorb anything as intangible as the future.

Elizabeth arranged for Nanny to take Charles on visits to other families, friends of hers, and all with several children in the family. By the time Anne arrived, Charles was quite familiar with the general idea of small boys having brothers and sisters. In one way Elizabeth was lucky in being able to prevent Charles from feeling the jealousy which most other children feel at being squeezed out of the center of their mother's affections by a second child. Elizabeth was always so busy at official duties that she only rarely saw Charles even at the best of times, and seldom for more than an hour a day in the evening. When Anne was born, Charles was so pleased at being able to see his mother around the house so much he soon forgot his surprise at his first sight of his sister.

It was almost like a holiday for Charles. His father was around, too, from Malta, and this was even better because Papa was always good for a knockabout game or a chat about boats and engines (Charles has always loved watching engines).

Next idea was to introduce Charles to Anne quickly. Anne was only a few weeks old, and Elizabeth just out of bed, when they let him sit on a sofa and hold his sister in his arms by himself. It was a nerve-wracking performance for everybody who watched, but one which Charles handled brilliantly and with great satisfaction.

From then on Charles was encouraged to feel that it was up to him to look after Anne and protect her. He helped to bathe her, comb her hair, and pick up the things she dropped. Alert photographers have often been able to take advantage of Charles' spontaneous affection for his sister, and have caught some wonderful shots. The first time was when Charles was caught bending over Anne's pram, kissing her on the cheek. A second was at Aberdeen, in Scotland, when Charles and Anne were on their way home to London from Balmoral Castle, and Charles in an American-styled T shirt, heaved his little sister up so she could see out of the window.

Nurse Lightbody had all sorts of tricks of her own to keep Charles contented and happy in Anne's company. When she began to take the children out together, she put Charles into a new pram, larger and more masculine than his old one, which was given to Anne. Just as she hoped, Charles felt that he had been promoted.

There was a secret cupboard at Clarence House, full of gifts from well-wishers all over the world. They were given to Charles one by one over a period of time, so that he would not be spoiled or lose his excitement for them. Every time Anne got a new toy, Nurse Lightbody unlocked the secret cupboard and gave him something especially colorful. So Charles never felt that Anne was getting more than he. The system worked so well that a few weeks before Elizabeth's Canadian tour he was asked to give Anne some of his old clothes and added to the pile, quite voluntarily, one of his favorite toys, a duck that squeaked; by which time Nurse Lightbody could boast that Charles had never had a day's jealousy of Anne in his life.

After a few rigid months during which Anne seemed

so bemused by the charm of her big brother that she forgot to make much progress herself, the baby girl suddenly caught up with herself and by her first birthday was able to say just as many words as Charles could at the same age. Ever since, Anne has been less placid than Charles but has never quite shown the little boy's vital curiosity. Like his father, Charles turned into a confirmed asker of questions. One famous barrister, a Queen's Counsellor, emerged exhausted some time ago from a stiff session under Charles' cross-examination as to who he was, what he was doing at the Palace, what was he carrying under his arm, etc. A delighted court official insists he heard the barrister mutter obscurely to himself as he left, "So *that's* how it feels!" But this may be apocryphal.

More than one visitor to his own subsequent remorse has become impatient with Charles' unstoppable stream of questions and replied sharply, but Elizabeth and Philip have never done so, and always answer everything as seriously and accurately as he could be expected to understand. The one thing which irritates *them* is any visitor using baby talk on either of the children.

The difference in temperament between Charles and Anne was partly due to the different circumstances in which they were born. When Charles arrived, Elizabeth was still the Empire's favorite daughter, the bride of only a year before, a girl who made the world feel old because it seemed such a little time since she was a child herself. By the time Anne came, Elizabeth was a settled and efficient young matron.

At the good age of one, Charles weighed twenty-five pounds. He received a birthday cake with icing in half a dozen colors and decorated with an icing bear, a crown, a lamb, a rabbit, and a squirrel holding a nut. He showed very little interest in most of his toys in that year, seeming to prefer an old wooden spoon and a saucepan, which he banged with agonizing concentration.

Like many small boys he learned to run before he could walk—or at least that was the way it seemed. He seldom cried, though more than one London mother cried for him as she saw the little fellow topple headlong on his way into St. James's Park, then stand plaintively but uncomplaining while Nanny wiped away slivers of sharp gravel from his knee with her crisp white handkerchief.

His favorite perpendicular sport was called "kick the ball," a wildly inaccurate form of soccer with rules which only Charles could understand and which he changed continually to shift the advantage of the game strategically to himself.

To the household staff Charles was "Charles" and not "Master Charles" as many British children would be called by the servants. In everyday conversation, though, many of the servants slipped into a habit that still persists in referring to him as "the little fellow."

A Teddy bear, growing steadily more battered, slept beside Charles at night throughout 1951, and on his walks he grew into the habit of pulling behind him an elephant on wheels. Those, of course, were the tastes of any small child. But there were habits, tastes, and ways which showed Charles to be the special fellow he is, a Royal Prince. By the time he was two and a half he knew the difference between a Life Guard and a Royal Horse Guard, which is more than many adults can do. During the ceremonies for the King's birthday in June, 1951, shortly before the King's second relapse, Charles was at Buckingham Palace before ten-thirty A.M. when his mother was taking the salute at the Trooping of the Color. He watched the whole parade and then the fly-past which did not end until one. Not once in those two and a half hours did his concentration waver. A long day for a baby, and one which made his father shake his head when he heard of it. Philip was not so much dubious about the tiring effect on Charles but by the feeling, disconcerting to any sailor, that his son was showing much more interest in the Army than he was in the Navy.

After marching and kicking footballs, Charles' favorite game in those days was hide-and-seek. He ruthlessly recruited any visitor who happened to call on his mother. Strangers reported that he would appear from nowhere, bow with superb courtesy, and without any sort of conversational preamble, say casually, "Will you play hide-and-seek with me?"

As one family friend commented to me at the time, "It's the kind of hide-and-seek where you have to take a *long* time finding him."

He later developed a shock-troop variant of the game by flying precipitately out of the nursery whenever the nursemaids' backs were turned. While they panted in pursuit he whizzed downstairs into the dining room or upstairs into the bedrooms, giggling gleefully when he was finally collared and hauled back to the nursery.

With girls Charles showed great confidence in his own charm. A pretty, blonde girl, aged two and a half, came to tea with him. He was her elder by a couple of months or so. While the two nannies watched at a distance, Charles, enchanted and wasting no time, tried to plant an affectionate kiss on a rosy cheek, but the little girl, profoundly unimpressed by the king-to-be, pushed him away. Charles was not discouraged in the slightest and tried again. The little girl pushed harder. He tried a third time and his defiant sweetheart, heaving with all the strength of virtue, sent Charles rolling off the sofa and onto the floor with a thump.

He looked around, startled, and saw the nannies suddenly deep in conversation with each other. Nobody came to help him. He got up and from then on kept the relationship to a strictly conversational plane.

Although he certainly had the vigor and the spirit to be as naughty as any other boy, Charles learned to curb himself more than most. The training from birth of royal children is so thorough that heavy punishment is hardly ever needed.

Whenever Elizabeth or Margaret were naughty as girls they were sent out of the room and made to apologize. Charles was trained from the beginning on similar lines. He was also given some concrete examples of what happened if he went too far. When he used to throw toys out of his pram they were picked up and returned to him—the first time. This he found excellent sport. When he made the play a second time the toy was picked up but not returned. This, thought Charles, was most unsportsmanlike; but neither argument nor Napoleonic brooding proved of any avail, so he drew the inevitable conclusion that grown-ups carried an irresistible might, and held on to his toys.

His grandparents, the King and Queen, were easier to deal with than his mother or Nanny. Like grandparents all over the world, they were much more inclined to spoil him. "He seems to get into everything," the present Queen Mother said breathlessly once after a romp through the rooms at Sandringham. Though officially he is not allowed much candy, the rules usually were forgotten whenever he visited Buckingham Palace. The secret came out one day when he appeared with his grandmother on the balcony at the Palace with a bulge in his cheek that could only be caused by toffee or toothache—with a celestial gleam in his eye revealing which it was. Charles has a very sweet tooth and he and his grandmother understand each other well.

From the beginning Charles and Anne wore as few clothes as the weather permitted, and neither of the two children was ever dosed with medicines. Nor was Charles ever put into a high feeding chair but always sat at a miniature table and chair of his own, eating correctly, British-style, with the fork in the left hand. The windows of the nursery were kept open winter and summer, and the children took their outdoor exercise in all weather except fog.

Charles quickly learned to enjoy listening to the radio and looking at books, but television quickly became his favorite. Whether Elizabeth, Philip, or anybody else likes the idea or not, he is a television baby and will be the first television Prince. Today Charles is getting his royal education on the family's sixteen-inch television screen. He watches every time his mother goes out on some televised function like the Trooping of the Color, and the lessons are teaching him what to do in the future. It will save him from much of the endless slog at constitutional training studies which his mother had to undergo for most of her childhood, and which his grandfather had to learn with infinite care and difficulty in middle age after ascending the throne unexpectedly on the abdication of Edward VIII.

He is pretty wise to life on the screen, though he was not always. Once on Philip's private screen, while he was watching newsreel movie shots of the party at Princess Anne's christening, he excitedly identified his father, mother, grandfather, grandmother, and great-grandmother, but did not recognize himself. When Philip, laughing, said, "It's you, Charles," he goggled at himself, first in disbelief, then in growing astonishment and finally with a satisfaction which bordered on the narcissistic.

Charles' day was not much different from that of other children. He awoke at six-thirty A.M. in time for orange juice. After Anne was born he was moved from the night nursery to a room of his own because he woke her up with his chattering. Orange juice and cod-liver oil were on ration in Britain and a nursemaid collected the ration every week from the local Food Office, using Charles' and Anne's special babies' ration books.

Breakfast was at eight. He usually ate a lightly cooked egg or grilled fish—a common English breakfast food—or cream cheese on toast. With it he had a raw apple and a mug of milk.

After breakfast and until ten-thirty Charles was left

to play in the nursery, joined whenever possible by his mother and father. Among the diversions other than Charles' proliferation of noise-making apparatus was a small climbing frame, a sandbox with a watering can, a large rubber ball about two thirds the size of a basketball, and wooden bricks.

By eleven A.M. he was officially presumed exhausted and laid in his pram, preferably in the garden near some shrubs or under trees so that he could hypnotize himself to sleep by watching them move. Nurse Lightbody did not mind if he did not sleep providing he rested.

Out of the pram he came at one-thirty for lunch, meat three times a week, fish twice. Sometimes he had liver or brains or egg all carefully cooked, the meat underdone, the brains peeled and boiled in milk, the liver grilled and shredded. He ate at least two vegetables, one green, at every lunch. For dessert he had boiled or steamed puddings which the English eat with relish, unmoved by their textural resemblance to paperweights.

At one-forty-five Charles took a walk—a royal caravan of babies, Nanny, nursemaids, and detective—into London's parks that became one of the sights of London. Security reasons put an end to it abruptly after the King's death, a wise move in view of the new, supreme position of Elizabeth, but rather a pity all the same. Teatime was at four-thirty. Waiting for him in the nursery when he got back

Charles usually found a glass of milk and a salad sandwich with shredded lettuce or seeded tomato or finely grated raw carrot. This was followed by brown bread and seedless jam, and a junket or milk jelly.

After tea he saw his mother, an eagerly awaited children's hour which showed by the state of Charles' excitement that loneliness, and the absence of a mother's constant care, is the one insuperable problem of royal children. Nothing can be done about it. The best that could be done has been done by Elizabeth who has kept her evening's hour with the children against nearly every pressure of business. After she became Queen she even altered the time of the monarch's weekly conference with the Prime Minister, so that Winston Churchill was instructed to make his call at six-thirty instead of five-thirty. Only when visits take her out of town or out of the country does Elizabeth let the children's hour pass. Together they played, or talked, usually quietly when Elizabeth visited him alone, though the sessions often turned into a romp if the King and Queen were present, as they usually were if Elizabeth and Charles were visiting them at the Royal residences of Sandringham, Windsor, or Balmoral.

Bath time was five-forty-five with the temperature of the water never more than 94 degrees. He cleaned his teeth himself and climbed into bed with a warm, sweetened drink. By six P.M. the small Prince's day was done.

Charles' wardrobe was large for a small boy. His clothes, chosen by Princess Elizabeth from the better London department stores, were gay and showed a keener eye for fashion than Elizabeth was doing at the time with her own clothes. Charles' appearance in a shirt and a slim bow tie practically revolutionized the fashion world of three-year-olds, and shortly afterward London and New York sprang out in a rash of infants in bow ties.

As for Anne, she had hardly any clothes at all to call her own. The awful secret came out when someone noticed that her white coat was buttoned up the wrong way, boy's style. It was obvious she was wearing a coat handed down from her brother. Anne's training was as old-fashioned as her wardrobe. Like Charles she was breast-fed and after she was weaned, Nurse Lightbody fed her with an ordinary feeding bottle.

Elizabeth and Philip did not like the thought of leaving them behind when they set out for Canada and the United States. The British and American newspapers which reported nearly every other detail connected with the private life of the Royal Family never seemed to discover that Elizabeth and Philip had never been able to live at home with their family for more than a few weeks in the three and a half years they had been married.

In September, 1951, another fact about the Royal Family which the newspapers had allowed themselves to forget returned to the headlines. It was not their fault, of course, that ever since the announcement of his illness in 1948 the King had done his best to minimize his critical condition and try to show himself to the best possible advantage whenever he was face to face with his subjects. But he could keep it secret for only so long. Buckingham Palace was forced to announce on the eve of Elizabeth's departure for Canada with Philip that King George VI had to undergo a major operation. The Royal Tour, now in its last stages of preparation, had to be postponed. After anxious conferences at the Palace with court advisers, doctors, the government, and Canadian officials, the King relentlessly overrode opposition and ordered his daughter and son-in-law to Canada to fulfill their obligations to the Dominion.

On October 8, only a week after schedule, and with the King showing little if any improvement, Princess Elizabeth and the Duke of Edinburgh left England. Instead of a comfortable crossing in the *Empress of Scotland*, they left by air and arrived at Dorval Airport, outside Montreal, after an all-night transatlantic flight.

Fifteen hours after they left England they stepped down from the plane in Canada. The Princess smiled her familiar smile. Philip threw his famous grin at the fainting teen-agers. This is what is known as *noblesse oblige*, or the customer is always entitled to expect the best from the Royal Family.

147

Your housewife in her small apartment with her factious children and her inadequate bank balance has her troubles. But only a princess is forced to smile and shake hands and make speeches and keep her lipstick fresh by some invisible source of replenishment in front of millions of people while her father, literally tired to death, lived out the last weeks of his life three thousand miles away.

CHAPTER *EIGHT*

The visit which Elizabeth and Philip paid to Canada and the United States in the fall of 1951 may be remembered by future generations as the time when Princess Elizabeth became beautiful.

One moment she seemed to be a plump matron with a distressing habit of appearing to wear everything in the closet at once. Next moment she was a stunning creature who took the breath away from everyone who looked at her. How she did it is a story in itself. But the really extraordinary thing was that people did not seem to notice the gradual transition she was making, getting her weight down and putting her wardrobe in order, although they had plenty of opportunities considering the number of times she appeared in public. All they saw was "Elizabeth —before" and "Elizabeth—after."

The "before" period included the time she was married in 1947. Elizabeth was a wonderful bride but she was certainly not beautiful. In addition to a tendency, at the time, not to photograph well, she also looked gawky and ill at ease. Always a good eater, she had cheerfully eaten herself by 1950 to a state where she was twenty pounds overweight. And unfortunately the time when she was at her fattest coincided with the period in which her mother's influence on her clothes was at its height. As every woman knows, the present Queen Mother has always defied every law of current fashions, but it did not matter so much with her. She had a chubby charm that could carry it off. Elizabeth was too young, insufficiently bouncy, and could not.

It was all very upsetting. The Empire had on its hands a Princess it adored passionately but a Princess that was both overstuffed and overdressed. Newspaper criticisms of her clothes and her weight irked Elizabeth, but they were only natural. It was a matter of public Commonwealth concern. The Empire belongs to the Royal Family, and the Empire likes it that way. But if it was granted the right to love Princess Elizabeth as a daughter, it also had the right to wince when she appeared in public looking like an Edwardian vaudeville queen.

In 1951 Elizabeth started her diet, and it was not easy. Elizabeth loved her food with a great healthy love and ate a lot of it—with chocolates between meals. As a nonsmoker she did not have the assistance of nicotine to hold down the poundage, and her favorite sport was, frankly, watching horse racing, or watching Philip play polo.

But Elizabeth was determined, and being a young lady of iron determination, a fact that has become increasingly apparent since she has become Queen, she stuck at it. She went off starchy food and she took appetite-reducing pills, a blue pill for breakfast, a green pill at lunch, and a chocolate pill at dinner.

At the same time she admitted some of the truths of the photographs taken of her, so she cleared her mind of all preconceived ideas about clothes and put her wardrobe exclusively in the hands of Norman Hartnell, Hardy Amies, and one or two other good British designers. No longer did she offer her own suggestions for a bit of fur here or a bow there. She steeled herself to simplicity and turned down advice even from the family and friends.

It is widely believed that it was Philip who suggested Elizabeth should "reform," no pun intended. But this is not so. Philip was always silent on the matter. No girl likes to be reminded she is putting on weight—she always knows it herself—or that she dresses badly, and out of respect to his wife's feelings he never once criticized or chipped in with any gratuitous advice. It was all Elizabeth's own work. One or two newspapers did notice the gradual improvement in Elizabeth's shape, but, to all effects it was a completely new Elizabeth that emerged from the BOAC stratocruiser at Dorval Airport.

Her shoes were still wrong but that, too, was soon put right. The important thing was that Elizabeth had blossomed into the full beauty that up to that time had been largely latent. And from then until the present day she has been growing more and more and more and more beautiful. She looked lovely, if too grave, when she stepped off the plane. When she was photographed in Ottawa in a checked blouse and peasant skirt swinging gaily through "the Cattle in the Crop" she looked entrancing.

A few months later when the King died she was photographed in a car, wearing black, head averted, her eyes misty and unseeing, and it was one of the most beautiful pictures ever taken of a bereaved woman. Rembrandt might have painted it, but Bernhardt could never have acted it, and Vivien Leigh never looked as beautiful.

Ten months after that, in November, 1952, when she attended the State opening of Parliament, the United Press cameraman Charles Dawson took a picture of Elizabeth so radiant as almost to dazzle. Possibly this picture touched the ultimate in twentieth-century royal beauty. This was none of that beauty which is so dubiously called "ageless," often a euphemism to describe a face that might have looked beautiful in some epoch but doesn't any more. This was beauty on the Hollywood model, satisfying every standard that Hollywood has set, but braced and glorified by centuries of breeding and Christian ethics, and a lifetime of training in deportment and the knowledge of being universally loved.

Today the British Commonwealth of Nations has the

quite heady inspiration of knowing that one of the most beautiful women in the world is on its throne. The plain girl of twenty-one has become the world's number one glamour girl at twenty-six. The next question is how she will look at thirty and at forty. The chances are she will be lovelier than Dietrich or Garbo, because she is quite obviously one of those lucky women who grow more beautiful as they get older.

It was Elizabeth herself who made the trans-America tour something exceptional and superlative among royal tours. Otherwise it went more or less as expected, generally triumphant with a few blemishes here and there, the result of too much strain on the royal couple, and too much enthusiasm on the part of the people and the newspapermen.

Elizabeth and Philip had the original disadvantage of having to make up for a bad beginning, after the Canadian authorities were involved in a ridiculous flummox. Originally the royal visitors were scheduled to arrive at Quebec by sea. Instead, owing to the King's illness they arrived by airplane at Montreal.

The logical thing was to start the tour from Montreal but this needed rather more improvisation than could be absorbed easily by the bureaucratic mind. So the authorities decided to pretend it didn't happen. They planned to whisk Elizabeth and Philip hastily by car from Montreal to

Quebec—which meant going backward from the intended direction—and start the tour as originally conceived. Consequently the reception at Dorval was neither one thing nor the other. It was not really a reception at all. There was a committee and a lot of children waving Union Jacks and Quebec flags and a car waiting to take Elizabeth to Quebec, but nothing like the welcome that should have been accorded—and which Canadians intended to accord—to a future Queen of the Commonwealth.

The Princess, worried about her father, disconcerted by a bumpy flight, apprehensive at the first great responsibility she had to carry out away from the protection of her father and mother, was justifiably irritated at the snafu. Driving from the airport she stared unsmiling at the children who had been waiting for hours in freezing weather, and only Philip smiling handsomely and waving to everybody saved what might have been a noticeably bad impression.

No official explanation was forthcoming as to Elizabeth's distress, but officials let it be known that she had suffered from airsickness on the flight over. This was hardly a likely story. Elizabeth is a splendid sailor and has never known a moment's seasickness in her life, and people who do not suffer from seasickness rarely suffer from airsickness. They should have given out the more accurate story that

154

Elizabeth was irked at the lack of imagination shown by the Canadian officials.

In the end little damage was done. After twenty-four hours or so on Canadian soil the Elizabethan charm dawned like a sunrise and all was well. The other misadventures on the trip were of a minor character and generally understandable.

French Canada went wild, a fact that should have surprised nobody but did. It is well known that the French Canadians do not take comfortably their position in the Commonwealth, but whatever their discontent it has never involved the person of the monarch of England. The Crown has never become the symbol of opposition in Quebec in the way it has in Ireland. The French Canadians with their Gallic and definitely un-Irish logic have kept their attack concentrated chiefly on more tangible things like their encirclement by English Canadians and the domination of English wealth on St. James's Street which is Montreal's equivalent of New York's Wall Street, or London's City.

Even more harassing to French Canadians has been the increasing influence of the United States in Canadian affairs resulting in a greater isolation of the French population. The French were among the most vigorous opponents of such Canadian moves as the decision to end the Privy Council in London as the last forum of appeal in

Canadian legal disputes, and the still more recent decision to appoint a Canadian instead of an Englishman as Governor-General. Both these moves seemed to cut Quebec further and further adrift in the English-speaking continent.

This is an almost absurd simplification of a complex problem, but it helps to explain the overwhelming reception which Quebec gave to Elizabeth and Philip. Maurice Duplessis, the rabble-rousing Quebec Prime Minister, described Quebec to Elizabeth as "the synonym for loyalty" and he spoke from the heart.

At a State dinner in the Château Frontenac Elizabeth made her first official speech—in perfect French, a fact that enamored the French Canadians even more completely, the whole culture of the Province revolving as it does around its language and its church. And a good French accent charms the Canadians much more than, say, the King's English charms Americans or Australians.

A great weight of official functions crushed them at Quebec, but they managed them ably and were able to take a brief time out to relax in a hunting lodge at Ste Agathe. The press and the officials left them alone; even the public, with good manners contrasting vividly with the scenes in England after Elizabeth's wedding, stayed away and Philip was able to drive his wife in a horse-drawn sleigh through the byways of the Laurentian mountains.

In Ottawa Elizabeth and Philip sampled Alberta elk,

Saskatchewan grouse, Manitoba wild rice, and enjoyed much entertaining by the Canadian government. By now Elizabeth had managed to speak once or twice by transatlantic telephone to London, talked to Prince Charles, and learned that her father was feeling better. After that her step was unmistakably lighter.

As usual Philip was a sensational success even though his habit of wearing suède shoes, popular enough in England and Europe, raised the eyebrows of fashion-conscious men in America where suède is usually associated with zoot suits.

In Toronto Philip left his wife for the first time. He addressed a meeting of 1,700 businessmen while Elizabeth lunched with seventy-five young mothers at Parliament Buildings. Elizabeth and the girls listened by loud-speaker as Philip launched confidently into a confused eulogy of the Canadian achievement. It was almost unquotable, certainly not one of his better efforts, but it was rousingly applauded. Afterward Philip rejoined his wife who was still entertaining the mothers, and said feelingly to the assembled group, "Golly, you're prettier than the lot I've been talking to."

Philip lost his temper with photographers at Niagara, and with some justification. He and Elizabeth, clad in mackintoshes to avoid the spray of the falls, endured patiently a barrage of flash bulbs, and he, thinking it was all over, took his wife's arm to go. But one or two photographers—as one or two photographers always do in any cluster of their craft—wanted more photographs, and as Philip innocently turned his back, they muttered irascibly to themselves. Philip heard the complaints they uttered under their breaths and wheeled on them. "What are you belly-aching about now?" he demanded angrily, whereupon officials descended like a swarm of bees and ushered the photographers frantically away.

Everyone present was heartily on Philip's side. But Niagara on the whole was a happy experience. Elizabeth and Philip gazed in awe at the falls and 20,000 Canadian and American sight-seers gazed in awe at Elizabeth and Philip. But local statisticians were obliged to admit that, in the past, larger crowds had turned up to see people go over the falls in a barrel.

There was an incident of light relief when on the way from Niagara to Windsor, Ontario, the royal train had a false start. At St. Catherine's Elizabeth got off to chat to the mayor and local officials. A pipe band waited at attention to provide the musical background. Somewhere the signals got mixed. No sooner had the band piped up the first wails than the train started to move out. Elizabeth was still chatting on the platform and looked around, startled. Officials charged down the platform, risking heart and blood pressure, arms flailing and shouting, "No! No! Stop!" Baaaa! went the bagpipes.

Elizabeth went pink trying to hold down the giggles and after a few minutes the train chugged sheepishly back. Elizabeth got on it and waved good-by. Her loyal Canadian subjects waved dutifully until it disappeared from sight, then went into a huddle of blasphemous recriminations.

Winnipeg gave them a rousing welcome and out among the great plains reception followed reception. Far too much work was thrown on the couple and far too little protection was offered them against the excessive loyalty of the people. It was all heart-warming but Elizabeth and Philip just had too much to do, too many places to visit, people to meet, and wreaths to lay. What was needed was some member of the government who should have been attached to the party all the time, screening local requests for appearances and trying to arrange some greater variety of experience for the Princess and the Duke. In 1939 King George VI and Queen Elizabeth had McKenzie King, the Canadian Prime Minister, always at their side. But Louis St. Laurent, the Prime Minister at the time, was engaged in a political battle in Ottawa, and Elizabeth and Philip were more or less at the mercy of the local authorities.

For amusement Elizabeth and Philip turned from time to time to one of the "characters" in the party, an engaging

Montrealer named Cory Thompson, who was on a photographic assignment. Thompson's brand of humor was sometimes rather primitive, as when the party toured a grain elevator he filled his bowler hat with wheat. Passing Elizabeth he made a sweeping bow and an avalanche of wheat fell down his face. It was just what was wanted to relieve tension, and he became a great favorite in the party.

Out among the cowboys near Calgary, Thompson earned the cheers of the royal party. Seeing this innocuous young tenderfoot, wandering around aimlessly in a bowler hat and carrying an umbrella, one of the chuckling cowboys suggested that he might like to ride a horse grazing with suspicious docility inside a barred field.

Wide-eyed with innocence, Thompson agreed. Keeping his bowler hat on, he clambered clumsily on to the back of the horse which immediately convulsed with indignation. It bucked, reared, stood on two legs, dipped, rolled, yawed, and frothed. Thompson stayed on the horse. The bowler hat stayed on Thompson. The cowpunchers' mouths went open and Philip howled in joy. The spectators from the royal party, feeling that Thompson was one of them and striking a blow in their behalf, yelled their encouragement. The horse gave up first. With bad grace it conceded defeat and came to a standstill, and one of the finest horsemen in Canada—a former Cavalry champion—climbed down, picked up his umbrella, raised his hat to the cowboys, and walked away.

From Winnipeg Elizabeth and Philip traveled by road to Regina, Saskatchewan, where the local citizenry presented them with caribou slippers for the Princess and the children, and caribou gloves for Philip. Elizabeth spontaneously asked to see the Museum of the Royal Canadian Mounted Police who had guarded her with discreet efficiency throughout the tour so far and who were to stay with her until the end. After she had seen the museum, the mounties staged for her a first-class horse show.

At the halfway point the New York *Times* correspondent was able to cable, "All Canadians have found Elizabeth appealingly pretty and gently dignified, the correct combination both for the symbol of the crown and the prototype of a young mother. Most Canadians are hypnotized by the long publicity build-up for her tour and the coverage of the Canadian press, which pictures the royal visit as the public's date with history and glamour. The feeling in the Dominion can be summed up this way: the Empire's darling baby has grown up to be a credit to the family."

At Victoria in British Columbia both Elizabeth and Philip stopped off to go to the hairdresser's and an awful secret came out. Philip sat down and said warningly, "I don't want a crew cut. But I want it short. Don't leave it too long, whatever you do. I don't want to have to go to the barber's again until I get back to London."

The barber looked down, and there it was, a thin spot. Not a bald spot yet, but an ominous thinning out. He sighed at the perishability of the human body but he did not comment, consoling himself that it would be many years yet before the handsome Duke got appreciably bald.

Elizabeth had a happier time with her hairdresser who later confessed the Princess' hair was "lovely." Elizabeth admitted that she missed her children but confirmed hastily she was "loving the tour." While the hairdresser administered an oil shampoo she respectfully asked what impressed Her Highness most about Canada.

Elizabeth thought for a moment, then said, "the distances." After a while she added, "One hears about the vastness of Canada. One reads about it, but one's mind cannot grasp it until one spends seven nights in a train and *sees* it."

From British Columbia they began the train journey back, everywhere repeating their immense success. It was a tired couple that returned to Montreal on October 29, but Montreal stimulated her by giving the royal couple the most uproarious welcome of the tour, and Elizabeth's appearance at the floodlit balcony of the Windsor Hotel

162

in Dominion Square provided a magnificent climax to the trip. Afterward they went to relax at an ice hockey game before making preparations for the trip to the United States.

So gay and friendly were Elizabeth and Philip that no officials could begin to guess the weariness they were both feeling. In Montreal Philip, under some provocation, lost his temper again. Some unimaginative official decided that the members of the press should line up for a farewell handshake with Elizabeth and the Duke. Many of the correspondents were scheduled to follow the royal couple all the way to Washington and back to England, so they could hardly conceive it as a farewell gesture, and said so. Even more important, nearly all of them were close to their deadlines and were impatient to get their dispatches away.

But they were impressed into the ceremony by flustered functionaries who assured them that any change of plans would constitute a serious affront. The first glance at Elizabeth and Philip convinced the correspondents that such was not the case. Both were tired and strained and were just as irritated to have this function thrust on them as the correspondents.

The newspapermen swallowed their annoyance, but Philip did not. He shook a few hands perfunctorily and suddenly rebelled when face to face with John Hartley, correspondent of the London *Times*. Philip recognized him and exclaimed, "Aren't you coming back to England with us?"

"Yes, sir," said Hartley, startled, "I am."

"Then this is all a waste of time," said Philip and put his hands behind his back, refusing to shake hands with anyone else. Appearing not to notice her husband's sulks, Elizabeth became extra-sweet and shook every correspondent's hand vigorously. Philip had had a trying time, but the correspondents, hurt, felt he should not have taken it out on them. They had followed him in the close confinement of a press train all round Canada and some of them were on the verge of blows with one another anyway.

From Montreal they flew to Washington for the busiest, briefest trip ever made to the United States by a member of the Royal Family. President Truman was at the airport to greet her. He called her "my dear," and surprised Elizabeth by asking her to wait at the foot of the airplane until the cameramen had had their fill of photographs.

The President, from experience, knew what he was doing. While they stood together he lightened any tension that existed by whispering to her a few good-humored Truman wisecracks which made Elizabeth laugh and set her off to her best advantage for the photographers. Some of the pictures taken in Washington were the best of the trip.

Washington gave her one of the most enthusiastic and noisiest greetings of the tour. Her one big chore was to shake hands at the British Embassy with 1,500 prominent American guests. The mile-long queue started forming in the Embassy ballroom an hour and a half before Elizabeth was scheduled to arrive. Elizabeth had a word for everyone, but took time out halfway through for a cup of tea, made English-style without teabags. The guests proceeded from the Princess to the bar where champagne was being served, and everything went off splendidly. The only hold-up was caused by a seventeen-year-old Eagle Scout who had so many badges that Philip stopped to ask him about them.

The unusual part of the royal visit to Washington was that it was the first visit Elizabeth made to any city as a strictly Canadian Princess. It was the Canadian not the British flag which fluttered behind her, and the Canadian not the British Embassy which sponsored arrangements for her visit.

The Princess' last official duty was to present the President with two gifts for the renovated White House— both presents from King George—a pair of rare eighteenth-century English candelabra and a carved eighteenth-century gilt mirror.

In November the trip ended and the royal couple returned for a brief rest in England before setting out for Australia and New Zealand. Queen Elizabeth and Prince

Charles were waiting at Euston Station to greet them. Elizabeth and her mother embraced and kissed each other, but, as usual it was Charles who stole the show. He saluted as orders were shouted to the Guard of Honor, formed by the Second Battalion of the Coldstream Guards to present arms. But he jumped, startled, as the rifles were slapped to the shoulders and a hundred hands smacked on the rifle butts. He started again and slipped a hand cautiously into his mother's as the drums rolled for the beginning of the National Anthem.

Then he solemnly shook hands with the distinguished company of dignitaries who had come to the station to greet the Princess. Deadpan he greeted the Marquess of Salisbury, Lord Ismay, who was Secretary of State for Commonwealth Relations, Mr. Walter Gifford, the American ambassador, Mr. L. D. Wigress, High Commissioner for Canada, and Sir David Maxwell Fyfe, the Home Secretary. Afterward he escaped while his parents were chatting to the reception committee and challenged Major Lord Suffield, commanding the Guard of Honor. "Where's your sword?" he demanded, and the major, slightly embarrassed, showed the hilt protruding from the slit in his greatcoat. Charles was fascinated by the uniforms of the four Canadian Mounties who had served as a personal bodyguard of the Princess and the Duke in Canada, and peered closely at their red jackets and blue riding breeches.

As on Elizabeth's return from South Africa four years before, it was London who gave her the greatest reception of all, packing the West End and the Mall to cheer her home. The Royal Standard was broken once more over Clarence House.

But Elizabeth and Philip barely looked in and out of their own home. They drove straight to Buckingham Palace to see the King. He greeted them in his private suite and to their relief looked quite well. No one will ever know how determination could conquer physical condition to the extent that he was able to look fit and cheerful for his daughter's return. It was only a few weeks before they were off again. The King, haggard and bareheaded in the winter wind, saw them off for Australia in the airliner *Atalanta*.

The King's story was nearly over, but he was awaiting death without fear. "In the end," Churchill said later, "death came as a friend." Some weeks before he died, a farmer at Sandringham was stern with the hatless, coatless King who passed him by.

"Sir," ventured the farmer, "you should take more care of yourself in this weather."

The King replied, smiling, "I may not have very long to live, and I want to get about while I can."

He seemed in reasonable health, however, and in London preparations went on for the forthcoming health cruise which the King, the Queen, and Princess Margaret planned to make to South Africa at the invitation of the South African government.

While Margaret and Queen Elizabeth spent time at the Palace approving sketches of their wardrobe for the trip the King stayed at Sandringham shooting hares.

The day before he died was a particularly successful one for him. He returned in the evening with a bag of fifty hares, accompanied by Lord Fermoy, the Irish peer, and five other "guns."

"Who's coming again tomorrow?" he asked his six companions cheerfully as he said good night. After dinner Margaret played the piano for him while he worked with a jigsaw. Once she stopped playing to help him with an intricate assortment of pieces. The family went to bed early, leaving the King alone with a last cup of cocoa and a hunting magazine, and no one again saw him alive. He was discovered by a servant bringing him his morning cup of tea, dead of a heart attack.

Elizabeth was in Kenya when she became a Queen without knowing it. The evening before she had watched big game gather at a water hole in the Royal Aberdare Game Reserve. From among the trees a herd of fifty elephants lumbered out and Elizabeth, grasping Philip's arm hard—one of her characteristic habits in his company—began to laugh hysterically, "Philip!" she gasped. "They are pink! Pink elephants! I don't believe it." Actually the elephants were a good respectable elephant-gray but had been rolling in some pink dust in the forest. "How father would love this," she added.

Next day she climbed into a blouse and slacks, ate her usual hearty breakfast and, leaving the tree hut in which she had spent the night, started back with Philip, her staff and her hosts, for the lodge which had been given her as a wedding present by the people of Kenya.

All day the message of the King's death had been trying to get through by wire, but was for some inexplicable reason delayed. Not until the early afternoon did the news reach the lodge and even then it came indirectly, the editor of a local paper having called the lodge by phone.

Philip heard the news from an equerry and waited to consider how to break it. While Elizabeth was in another part of the house chatting gaily to Kenya officials he cabled London for confirmation. When the reply came he took Elizabeth for a walk and broke the news to her alone.

Within a matter of hours they were on their way back 4,000 miles to a new life. Elizabeth's composure never deserted her. She wrote notes of regret to every organization waiting to greet and entertain her, and her last act before boarding the plane was to offer her lodge to a recently married Kenya official for his honeymoon.

The weather in London at four-twenty-nine P.M. on

February 7, 1952, was suitably filthy, contrasting almost symbolically with the tropical sunshine Elizabeth had left behind her in Africa.

A reception committee waited at the airport. The Duke and Duchess of Gloucester were there, and so were the Earl and Countess Mountbatten and members of the government and opposition. Winston Churchill moodily drew figures with his walking stick in the gravel, and Clement Attlee, who had been the King's Prime Minister for even longer than Churchill, stood fidgeting, gray-faced and tense. The others waited impassively.

The plane landed one minute ahead of time and for the fourteenth time in four months Elizabeth alighted on the tarmac. She was pale but dry-eyed, wearing a hastily purchased black coat lightened only by a *diamante* brooch. She was kissed on the cheek by the Gloucesters and Mountbattens. Tears ran down Churchill's cheeks as he tried— with rare incoherence for him—to find words to combine welcome, sorrow, and a new reverence.

Almost impatiently the new Queen turned to Lord Woolton and remarked that it had been a good trip, "a tragic homecoming, but a smooth flight." The plane's crew were lined up and Elizabeth remembered to thank each in turn, then, stepping into the family Daimler, drove with Philip to Clarence House. Queen Mary as erect as ever was there to greet her. The Queen Mother and Princess Margaret were still at Sandringham attending to funeral arrangements, and Elizabeth called them by telephone. Margaret broke down but the Queen and the Queen Mother remained calm. Twenty-six hours after the King's death there was still no time for tears.

As Elizabeth put the telephone down, Sir Alan "Tommy" Lascelles, Private Secretary to the King for the past nine years, begged audience.

"In your office, Ma'am," he said, almost apologetically, "the boxes."

The "boxes" were containers holding state papers, confidential messages, telegrams, foreign dispatches, letters of royal appointment, all documents requiring either the monarch's perusal or the monarch's signature. There were special red boxes from the Foreign Office with messages so secret that only the monarch may read them, and no secretary is allowed to digest them down to manageable size.

It was now the Queen's job to attend to them. In British constitutional procedure there is no escape from the boxes, because British government is conducted in the Queen's name and without her signature the machinery of government would stop. There are only two ways a reigning monarch can get away from the boxes. One is by dying, as even kings must do, or by going mad, as kings have done. George III, for example, did, leaving the business of kingship to a regent.

Nothing stops the flow of boxes twice a day seven days a week. The new Queen set to work. It was another day before she could escape to Sandringham, see her father and family, and for the first time, be left alone with her grief.

 CHAPTER *NINE*

The impact of the new reign was felt even more quickly than people expected. The monarchy, always beloved, became suddenly a thing of tremendous excitement.

Elizabeth's accession was formally proclaimed in a blaze of medieval pageantry from four points in London with the central point in St. James's Palace. There Sir George Bellew, the Garter Principal King of Arms, standing in a red and golden cascade of such royal officials as the Earl Marshal (the Duke of Norfolk), two more Kings of Arms, six Heralds, and three heraldic Pursuivants, raised a large parchment and declared sonorously:

"Whereas it has pleased Almighty God to call to His Mercy our late sovereign lord King George VI, of blessed and glorious memory, by whose decease the Crown is solely and rightfully come to the high and mighty Princess Elizabeth Alexandra Mary, we therefore, Lords Spiritual and Temporal of this realm, do hereby with one voice and consent of tongue and heart publish and proclaim the high and mighty Princess Elizabeth Alexandra Mary is now become Queen Elizabeth II by the Grace of God, Queen of this realm and all her other realms and territories, head

173

of the Commonwealth, Defender of the Faith to whom her lieges do acknowledge all faith and constant obedience with hearty and humble affection; beseeching God by Whom kings and queens do reign to bless the royal Princess Elizabeth II with long and happy years to reign over us. God Save the Queen."

Elizabeth II became the sixth reigning queen of England and easily the most beautiful. Her predecessors were the sour and vicious Mary I (1553-1558) who died loathed by the British people and marked by the nickname, "Bloody Mary," which has lived through the ages; Elizabeth I, the present queen's illustrious namesake who came to the throne at the same age, twenty-five, in 1558 and ruled through nearly half a century of England's most glorious years; Mary II (1689-1694) the undistinguished, unlovely, uninspiring woman who reigned as coruler with her husband William; puffy, dropsical Queen Anne (1702-1714) whose claim to fame was having among her subjects the Duke of Marlborough, Winston Churchill's brilliant ancestor, and a bevy of architects who created a delightful era in building; and the incomparable Queen Victoria who ruled a fabulous Empire from 1837 to 1901.

Few people know today that Elizabeth might have been proclaimed Elizabeth III and not Elizabeth II, and if she had it would all have been the doing of Sir Walter Scott, the Scottish novelist. Sir Walter was being entertained to dinner one night in 1828 at the home of Princess Victoria Mary Louisa, the Duchess of Kent, and was presented to her daughter Princess Alexandrina Victoria of Kent, as Victoria was then called. The eminent writer winced when he heard her name and said he hoped she would not take the name of Victoria, if and when she became Queen. "Personally," he said, "I hope they will change her name to Elizabeth—Elizabeth II." The Duchess and all the other guests cooed agreement, but Victoria put her foot down in the way that only Victoria could, and would have none of it.

So the II it was for Elizabeth, except in Scotland where the northern citizens fought a brisk skirmish to try and prove Elizabeth was Elizabeth I of Scotland, they declining to accept responsibility for the Elizabeth who rolled the head of Mary Queen of Scots in the dust.

For the time-being, however, such problems were put aside for the future and Scotland, too, mourned its dead king. At Sandringham a pipe major played a Scottish lament as estate carpenters fashioned a coffin out of a neighboring oak, and the King's bier was carried to the local parish church where it lay in state for two days. After-ward it was taken to Westminster Hall in London.

In the funeral cortege that paced through the London streets in a cold, white February sunlight, the King's kins-men walked silently with their own thoughts.

There was the Duke of Gloucester, mournful and jowly, bewildered at the march of events that had left his life alone untouched amid the drama of his three brothers, two now dead and one exiled. There was Earl Mountbatten of Burma. Was he aware of the eyes on him from people who considered him the irresistible influence on Philip's life, and consequently on Elizabeth's life, and consequently on the throne itself?

Behind walked the frozen-faced Duke of Norfolk, Premier Earl and Earl Marshal of England, the man whose traditional job it was to crown English kings as they came to the throne and bury them when they died. His one love was horse racing, his one talent was his genius in organizing British pageantry on a scale and perfection to stagger Hollywood. This was his work, the slow march of the gray and the black, the roll of muffled drums, the rhythmic thud of soldiers' boots and clop of horses' hoofs, this superbly stark portrayal of the history that is signified when a king dies. In 1937, when he was not even thirty, Norfolk organized the Coronation of King George VI. Very shortly he would have to do the same for Queen Elizabeth II.

In the procession, too, was the seventeen-year-old Duke of Kent, alone in civilian clothes, his silk hat at a crazy tilt which drew comments. One day soon this boy would be attracting all the publicity that once belonged to Princess Margaret and the Duke of Windsor . . . the Duke of

176

Windsor, there too, in naval uniform, handsomely haggard and near him the man who most closely resembles him in all the Royal Family, Prince Philip, Duke of Edinburgh.

What did the future hold for Philip?

Prince Albert of Saxe-Coburg-Gotha, Philip's great-great grandfather, and the husband of Queen Victoria, once wrote of his duties, "The position of Prince Consort requires that the husband should entirely sink his own individual existence in that of his wife; that he should aim at no power by himself or for himself; should shun all attention, assume no separate responsibility before the public."

But times and personalities had changed. Philip was as unlike Albert in temperament as it was possible to be. On the other hand Philip and the Duke of Windsor were alike in many ways, in their tolerant attitude toward humanity, in their informality, in their irritation at the stuffier conceits of the Court. But the Duke of Windsor had been a King and his great play to buck tradition had ended in disaster. Philip could not move empires, and his hands were freer.

In the days, weeks, and months that followed, the pattern began to show through, with Philip first concentrating exclusively on taking as much worry as possible off his wife's shoulders, and then developing a philosophy of his own about the position of a queen's consort. After his return from Kenya, Philip worked night and day greeting and accommodating all the visiting princes and statesmen who poured into London for the funeral. When it was all over, he protectively rounded up the new Queen and the grieving Queen Mother and took them to Windsor for a few days' rest.

Next—regretfully—he turned to the business of packing up at Clarence House for the removal to Buckingham Palace. Philip loved Clarence House, and he had poured his heart into its renovation. He and Elizabeth had owned the place since mid-1950, but the call of naval and royal duties had been so intense that after eighteen months they could hardly look back on a week in which they had lived there uninterruptedly, and not more than a few weeks in all.

Although it was several months before they could expect to move to the Palace, Clarence House now ceased to be anything even faintly resembling a home. It was bedlam. The place seemed to be alive with diplomats, courtiers, and cabinet ministers. There seemed hardly to be a room which was not holding a conference, a council, or some royal appointment or other, and Philip reached the point where he started to take refuge in the grounds, meeting his own staff and even doing some of his business there.

Philip was certainly not being left out in the cold, but it was quickly seen that the new reign would be Elizabeth's and nobody else's, and that Philip would fit into the Elizabethan mold rather than vice versa.

For a few days there was some agitation in the Court as to whether the name of the dynasty from Prince Charles onward would be changed from Windsor to Mountbatten, in view of the fact that Mountbatten was Philip's and Charles' surname. This idea was quickly squashed by Elizabeth who announced that Charles would be a Windsor when he came to the throne. There was no controversy about the matter but it did have importance in Court politics.

The rumor-mongers who tried to make out the Mountbattens as the power behind the throne underestimated Elizabeth, and underestimated, too, the Mountbattens whose devotion to Philip and Elizabeth had been illustrated and proven on many occasions throughout both of the young couple's lives.

Even if Earl Mountbatten did have such aims he was at a great physical disadvantage. One of his ambitions for years had been to become Commander-in-Chief of the Mediterranean Fleet, and finally the slow-moving Admiralty appointed him to the post in May, 1952. But this meant he would be away from London for most of the first two years of Elizabeth's reign, a period when influence, if it was to be applied, would be most effective.

The moral tone of Elizabeth's reign would also follow

the Queen's own rigid sense of the proprieties and not assume Philip's more casual character. Back in 1949 Elizabeth firmly established her own ideas about life at a meeting of the British Mothers' Union.

"Some of the very principles on which the family and therefore the health of the nation is founded are in danger," she said speaking with a directness rare in royalty. "We live in an age of growing self-indulgence, of hardening materialism, of falling moral standards. There will always be unhappy marriages, especially when, as in time of war and of housing shortages, it is difficult for people to live normal married lives. But when we see around us the havoc which has been wrought—above all among children—by the break-up of homes, we can have no doubt that divorce and separation are responsible for some of the darkest evils in our society today.

"I do not think you can perform any finer service than to help maintain the Christian doctrine that the relation of husband and wife is a permanent one, not to be lightly broken because of difficulties or quarrels. I believe there is a far greater fear in our generation of being labeled priggish. In consequence people are sometimes afraid to show disapproval of what they know to be wrong, and thus end by seeming to condone what in their hearts they dislike. I am sure that it is just as wrong to err on that side as it is to be intolerant or overcritical."

180

In addition to revealing a highly aggressive sense of virtue, the statement suggested that the Duke of Windsor would not have much more success in getting the Duchess accepted by the new regime than he had done with the old, though the outlook for the Windsors might improve once old Queen Mary died.

These instances marked out the area of Elizabeth's rule where Prince Philip would not be allowed to invade. On the other hand, in the four years before the death of King George he had done a wonderful job in creating for Elizabeth a link with a world of which she had no knowledge or experience, but for which she had always had a tormenting curiosity. Now as consort to the Queen he could widen her horizon even further. He was thoroughly European in his education and could counter the isolationist tendency of the British Court, a tendency which even went so deep as to keep the Greek-born Duchess of Kent somewhat at arm's length during the King's reign.

Princess Marina always had a good friend in Queen Mary, but her experiences with the rest of the Court were not particularly warm after her husband's death, and like Princess Margaret later, she found her chief interests and friendships in the world of the theater and music. She is much more part of the Court circle today. On her return from her triumphant visit to Malaya in the winter of 1952, she was picked up in Malta by Philip himself, who was visiting the Mountbattens for a week, and they flew together to London where the Queen was waiting to meet them.

Philip, who is a cousin of the Duchess of Kent, is more closely related to the royal families of Europe than Elizabeth, with particularly intimate relationships among the royal houses of Greece, Denmark, and Sweden, and strong family ties with the German nobility. These ties would be likely to give the new British reign a more internationalist flavor than any it had known since Victoria's day.

So far, so good. Philip and Elizabeth today are a glamorous couple who balance each other's personalities nicely. If Elizabeth is the remote, regal Queen, Philip is her other self, friendly, accessible, and above all, human. Even his quite frequent outbursts of bad temper don't do him discredit. He is always resentful of attempts either by officials or the press to take advantage of Elizabeth's strict sense of duty. Sometimes he is powerless to do anything about it and seethes to himself as he stands a few feet behind his wife. But when he can act, he does so, sometimes, as in Montreal, to Elizabeth's embarrassment.

Philip's greatest gift is his ability to be both royal and informal at the same time. When he is called to the company of debutantes or women generally, his manner is the just-right combination of remoteness and familiarity. "Relax, girls," were his first words when he was introduced to some of Britain's women athletes at the 1952 Olympic Games in Helsinki. And he has been heard to call his wife a "silly sausage," with humorous exasperation after a private argument, an expression which did not appear to upset Elizabeth in any way.

For years Philip defied attempts by London's male fashion designers to make him a leader of fashion in the old Prince of Wales manner. Although Philip always looks smart he is not really interested in clothes. When he has a suit made he swings his arms through a full circle to make sure that it fits comfortably, and he does not ask much beyond that. He prefers suède to leather shoes, and cares little how battered they get. He loathes hats.

In spite of his efforts to avoid the suits and trappings of royalty, he is having to yield in many directions, and there is nothing he can do about it. The British people, used to seeing its royalty in the most glittering of uniforms, fell in love with Philip when they saw him as a simple naval lieutenant, mixing by virtue of his position as Elizabeth's husband, with admirals, generals, and diplomats, often looking excusably ill at ease among such a welter of decorations, orders, sashes, brass, and scrambled eggs.

At the time of writing he is a Commander in the Royal Navy with three gold rings on his sleeve and gold leaf on his naval cap. In time, of course, his position will oblige the Court and the Admiralty to make him an Admiral and the simple lieutenant will become like all the other princes, distinguishable from the rest of royalty only by his personality.

He has finally been forced by his high position into wearing the symbol of the upper-class Englishman, the bowler hat. But it is not hard to see Philip's distaste. He is nearly always seen carrying it in his hand. It is rarely on his head.

Philip has learned to fly in order to qualify for the honor of wearing RAF wings. All over the world "fly-boys" have a habit of waxing rather ironical about those bare-breasted officers who wear no wings and do ground-work in the service. For this reason it has always been presumed undignified for royalty to appear in RAF uniform without the wings. But kings and princes have too many other duties to be able to go through the whole flying course, so it has tended to become something of a formality. Philip was determined to make it less of one.

At first Air Force authorities at White Waltham, Berkshire, where Philip was getting his instructions, took careful precautions for his—and other people's—safety. An order was posted saying, "No plane may leave the airfield or come in while the Duke is in the air unless special permission is given."

But Philip was soon impatient with these precautions and insisted on going up in his little Chipmunk plane even when his instructors protested that the weather was not suitable. Philip's reputation spread. An English vaudeville star giving a performance at a special Christmas staff party at Windsor Castle, looked out of the corner of his eye at the Queen and apologized for being late. "We'd have flown in," he said, "but we were told the flying wasn't too safe in these parts . . . too many Chipmunks" (laughter).

Many people believed that the accession of Elizabeth as Queen would signify a general loosening-up in matters of protocol, but quite the opposite has happened. Elizabeth insists that every form and tradition relating to the dignity and supremacy of the Crown be maintained to the very letter.

A look into one of the diplomatic parties which she has given at Buckingham Palace gives a good picture of Elizabeth's type of Queenship. All the ambassadors and their aides are invited by gold-crested invitation from the Lord Chamberlain "on the command of Her Majesty." Shortly afterward, just so that nobody drops any bricks, Buckingham Palace issues a full set of instructions, worded something like this:

"Her Majesty's Marshal of the Diplomatic Corps presents his compliments to the Ambassadors and Chargés d'Affaires, and has the honor to inform them that the following will be the procedure at the Evening Party. Heads of Missions, together with the Ladies and Gentlemen of their Embassies and Legations, are asked to be good enough to arrive at the Entree Entrance. All other members of the Diplomatic Corps are asked to arrive at the Grand Entrance. The guests are asked to proceed up the Grand Staircase and to assemble as shown."

The instructions include directions to the powder room and to a first-aid station considerately set up in case the excitement of the occasion proves too much for the guests. Foreign legations are presented to the Queen not in order of importance but in seniority—an arrangement which, quaintly, makes the *doyen* of ambassadors the Chilean representative, Señor Don Manuel Bianchi, who has been in London since 1939, while at the bottom of the list is Winthrop W. Aldrich, United States ambassador since 1953.

All the guests are ordered to assemble separately in various State apartments before joining in the ballroom, and to be ready when the Queen enters. The guests go up the Grand Staircase, no one being announced. Almost a thousand guests attended the first diplomatic party, the Queen in advance letting an equerry know whom she wishes to chat to. The intermediary passes the word along quite informally just to make sure that those so favored stand near the dais in the ballroom and do not keep the Queen waiting. While the presentations are being made smoking is forbidden and there is no drinking, but music comes from a Guards band. Everywhere there are uniforms—Palace uniforms, Army uniforms, and diplomatic uniforms bright with orders.

The Queen passes through the State apartments with Philip at her side and members of her family like the Duke and Duchess of Gloucester, the Duchess of Kent, and the Princess Royal following behind. The women curtsey and the men bow deeply. Afterward all the guests assemble in the Palace ballroom where a Guards band is playing soft music and a champagne and buffet supper bar tempts the guests to the smoking room.

To those who are being received, the Queen extends her gloved hand and the person concerned touches lightly the tips of her fingers. The Queen always leads the conversation and manages it adroitly, nearly always succeeding in putting her guest at ease, though Philip is invaluable in smoothing sticky conversations in his usual cheery way. The conversations switch from language to language, Elizabeth falling into German and French where necessary, without difficulty, Philip following, though less happily. Nearby, Winston Churchill stands, cigarless but proud of his Queen, and beaming broadly.

Elizabeth who arrives at the party at nine-thirty,

187

exactly, usually leaves at about midnight. She has so far agreed to continue the relaxation of Court etiquette which now permits guests to leave the party before she does, and to turn their back on her on certain occasions. The former was instituted out of consideration for elderly guests; the latter to save some people from falling flat on their backs. In Queen Victoria's time all steps from the dais had to be negotiated gingerly in a reverse direction so that no common back was ever in Her Majesty's face, but now Elizabeth indicates when her chat is over by looking away and the guest is allowed to turn and walk from her.

What is it that people notice chiefly about the Queen at these parties? Her beauty? Usually. Her charm? Usually. But invariably the aspect that everyone notices is that during the two and a half hours she spends at the party she never takes a moment off to relax or even partakes of the champagne. Yet she never shows the slightest strain.

Some time before the Coronation a former Conservative member of Parliament was included in the train of royal automobiles which took the Queen from an official function in Manchester to another official function in Liverpool thirty miles away. It was part of a series of similar functions the new Queen was making in many parts of the country, and the ex-M.P. talked about it later in his club to a friend.

"I had made the same trip myself about twenty-five years ago and in circumstances not dissimilar," he said.

"Like the Queen I had to appear before audiences and make a speech in both places. I remember I managed to snatch a nap and look over my notes in the train between stations, but at the end of the day, believe me, I was really exhausted.

"The Queen also had to make speeches in both places, but the difference was that she could not relax in between. Not even in the car. The road was lined with people and there were thousands of school kids waving Union Jacks. She had to sit up and wave and smile to them all the time. My wife noticed that she did not get a single chance to look at herself in a mirror or powder her nose or use her lipstick. Then, when she got out at Liverpool, you can imagine it. Mayors, councilors, worthy local burghers, more Union Jacks, more kids than you would believe existed in such a small country. She had to stand and talk and shake hands for hours. Yet nobody expected her to look tired. I suppose they would have felt cheated if she *had* looked tired. I remember thinking to myself, in fact, that if she looked tired I would have been disappointed in her."

"And did she look tired?" inquired the friend anxiously.

"She looked as fresh as a daisy. I swear if an election had depended on it, I couldn't have done it."

That is an example of the strength of Elizabeth's constitution and mind. In the first few months of her reign the British people became worried at the back-breaking

189

schedule which she immediately assumed. Just as in America where the physical condition of presidential aspirants has become a matter of major importance, so it was in Britain where work had already killed a King, and the weight of constitutional responsibility seemed quite awful when one looked at it in print.

After King George's death a storm broke over his treatment. He had been under the care of a committee of eminent British doctors, not one of whom, however, had overriding authority over the others. Some medical circles felt that the King would have had more efficient medical care during the long period of his lung trouble if other arrangements had been made.

Anxiety over Elizabeth became so great that the *Lancet* magazine, normally a highly readable journal devoted to medical affairs, let out a burst of rare pomposity when it heard her schedule. "As the mother of a young family and the mistress of a home," the *Lancet* thundered, "the Queen has a life of her own whose happy fulfilment her subjects would place first. As doctors we should have special reason to welcome an assurance that by deliberate decisions taken in advance Her Majesty's health and vitality will be protected from her hereditary sense of duty."

Where the *Lancet* goes wrong is in imagining Elizabeth as a poor girl bearing up bravely under an intolerable burden of work. Actually, Elizabeth, like any other successful career woman, is stimulated by her work and enjoys talking shop with her mother or her husband more than anything else.

Her training has been too long and too careful to tire her seriously, and she gets no more weary than, for example, an experienced actress playing a demanding part or a big business executive after a long day at the office. She gets through her work twice as fast as the King used to do, because the King was caught unprepared for the job in middle age, and she handles her responsibilities with more assurance, though with less bounce than Philip, who never realized in his youth that this was going to be his career.

Philip's great achievement has been his capacity to link the Crown and the people across a wide expanse. The gulf was too deep for the Duke of Windsor, but Philip's position enables him to span it. He has done a tremendous job for the nation's underprivileged youth, who, thanks to his tireless efforts on their behalf, now enjoy far better sporting and recreational facilities than the average Ameriican city boy. Every day he calls the National Playing Fields Association to demand, "How much did we get in today? Not good enough. I'll have to do something about it."

And when the committee meetings begin to wander off the point as committee meetings often do, Philip would pull them back into line with a sailor's smartness. "That's not important," he would say, "what we want is more playing fields, and what I want to know is, how are we going to get them?"

From the bottom and from the top he has given a traditionally sporting people a still new enthusiasm for sport. For the slum urchin he has provided new playing fields and sports equipment, and from the aristocracy he has taken the sport of polo—one of his favorite sports—and given it something of a mass appeal.

He has had this most snobbish of all sports televised through the BBC, and quite large crowds are turning up in the south of England to watch the games—in fact several impoverished English noblemen have discovered a new source of income to keep their stately homes from falling down by charging admission to polo games on their grounds. Cowdray Park in Sussex has become especially popular, the lovely background of trees and the staccato thunder of horses' hoofs on turf providing a thrilling picture, though it must be confessed that Cowdray attracts the biggest crowds chiefly because fans want to see Philip in the rather sweaty flesh, as well as Earl Mountbatten and Billy Wallace, the ex-boy friend of Princess Margaret.

Philip has worked hard to cut down the expense of royalty by running economy campaigns at Buckingham Palace, the Queen's allowance of $1,330,000 a year, though not to be sniffed at, being none too large to cover the expense of the spectacular royal estates.

Philip has also managed to take over a huge amount of work that would otherwise have fallen on the Queen. At his own suggestion he was made Chairman of the Coronation Commission, and he took the worries of that enormous ceremony almost completely away from his wife. And he works so strenuously at the more rugged official engagements that the Queen's advisers sometimes wonder with cold perspiration what she would ever have done without him.

His manner at such tasks is always a model of tact and good taste, and many people have found it a good idea to take royal problems to him rather than to the Queen. His decisions are always made in the name of his wife. "I know the Queen won't like that," he says. "I think the Queen will want it done this way." This incidentally shows how completely Philip understands his wife, because Elizabeth has already proved herself not a person to be by-passed or fobbed off with generalities. Winston Churchill has discovered that, at their weekly conference, Elizabeth's questions on the affairs of the day are considerably more searching than those of her father.

The Queen has shown her appreciation of her husband's efforts by gratefully giving him a shove up the social ladder. In September, 1952, it was announced,

"The Queen has been graciously pleased . . . to declare and ordain that His Royal Highness Philip Duke of Edinburgh, Knight of the Most Noble Order of the Garter, Knight of the Most Ancient and Most Noble Order of the Thistle, Commander in the Royal Navy, shall henceforth upon all occasions and in all Meetings except where otherwise provided by Act of Parliament, have, hold and enjoy Place, Pre-eminence, and Precedence next to Her Majesty."

This made Philip First Gentleman of the land and gave him some of the authority he needed to add bite to his business. Until then Philip was regarded as a junior Duke and ranking even behind his own son, Prince Charles, who, as Heir Apparent, was titular First Gentleman. He was also ranked behind the Dukes of Windsor and Gloucester which could be embarrassing at functions like, say, banquets where the seating is strictly according to rank and seniority.

Elizabeth's order was a loving one in other ways. It meant that her husband who could never be King ranked superior to a man who had been King once (the Duke of Windsor) and the young man who would be King one day in the future—Prince Charles.

The change made the transition complete. Philip the young and the fair was now the next person in importance in the Commonwealth after the Queen. To get into the Court the atmosphere he most enjoyed, he now completed his staff which was tough, irreverent, and used to the sound of both bullets and oaths.

As a means of illustrating the type of place Buckingham Palace is today, some of the members of this staff are worth a longer look.

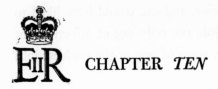 CHAPTER *TEN*

No ax falls on a British Court when a King dies the way it does on an American administration after a change of government, but the effect is the same.

One by one the old servants depart to their estates to tend to their Friesian cattle if they are farmers or write their memoirs if they are of a more literary turn; and bright new men from the armed services or universities move in to take their place.

The present regime is very bright and very new. In fact the departure of the old Lord Chamberlain and the arrival of the new might have looked right out of one of those Hollywood movies which C. Aubrey Smith used to make, with the affable, modern Earl of Scarborough moving in to take the place of the stooped, bearded, outgoing Earl of Clarendon.

Clarendon was a great figure in Buckingham Palace. He had been Lord Chamberlain there since 1938, and in his gray frockcoat at the side of King George VI at official functions and garden parties he was almost as well known to subscribers of the London picture magazines and newspapers as the King himself. All Elizabeth's life he had been a good friend and counselor, and she would have liked to keep the old man at his job, not only out of affection but also for his wisdom in the ways of one of the trickiest jobs in the Royal Household.

But Clarendon personally asked permission to bow out. At seventy-five, and with a Coronation coming up, he felt the job should go to a younger man, and in came the Earl of Scarborough, fifty-six years old, one of the nation's leading freemasons and a Yorkshire squire, with a nice, old-fashioned sense of justice. A couple of young ragamuffins invaded his estate to hunt mushrooms not long ago, and found a gold cigarette case and one or two other items that had been stolen from his home the year before. Scarborough, in delight, sat the lads down at the kitchen table and stuffed them to the brim with roast chicken, apple tart, and ice cream.

The Lord Chamberlain decides on Court ceremonial, watches matters of precedence, and advises the Queen on which people she shall invite to the Court and which people she shall not. He also issues Royal Warrants to deserving tradesmen and shopkeepers (giving them the right to carry the Royal Coat of Arms over their shop door, a right worth a fortune in prestige and publicity), and censors the plays that appear on the London stage. Theatrical censorship in England used to madden George Bernard Shaw and still maddens one or two contemporary playwrights, but it has always been used with a very light hand, as anyone who frequents the London theater can see, and the indications are that Scarborough will be just as broadminded in his outlook as his predecessors.

He is likely to be less so on another pressing problem which comes inside his jurisdiction on what to do about divorced people being invited to Court.

As protocol stands, some of the so-called "innocent" parties may be invited to Court, but only under certain circumstances of a nature so vague that it would be impossible to define in advance who would and who would not be eligible. Divorced members of the government—Anthony Eden for example—are automatically invited, simply because they are Ministers of the Queen, but otherwise the decision rests with the Lord Chamberlain.

The wretched business crops up also at the Ascot races where Queen Elizabeth has put her foot down hard and insisted that the traditional rule barring divorced persons from the Royal Enclosure must be rigorously upheld. The duty of sending out invitations falls on the Duke of Norfolk, who is a Catholic, and he works closely with the Lord Chamberlain to present a united front.

Whatever the rights and wrongs of the matter, it often gives onlookers from the common herd at Ascot much cause for amusement. Ascot is the most fashionable race meeting in the world. The gentlemen look resplendent in toppers and gray morning coats, and the ladies battle the capricious English weather with English determination, hanging desperately on to their Easter Parade hats through the squalls of wind. It is a common sight at Ascot to see two toppered and immaculate gentlemen chatting cheerfully to one another across the rail which separates the Royal Enclosure from the main stands, the one outside being a divorced man, and the one inside, respectable.

And every year through the Ascot season, estranged couples in Britain's social register bare their teeth at each other in the pretense of marital smiles, determined to delay divorce proceedings until after Ascot is over because they do not wish to miss the fun in the Royal Enclosure. This has been particularly true in the 1953 Coronation year.

If Scarborough for Clarendon represents the most important change in England's Court, the most glamorous new figure at Buckingham Palace today, apart from Philip himself, is Lieutenant General Sir Frederick "Boy" Browning, K.B.E., treasurer to the Duke of Edinburgh, husband of the best-selling novelist Daphne du Maurier, and listed by one English newspaper in 1952 as among the six most handsome men in England.

Browning acquired his nickname because of his swift rise through the Guards. He acquired his eminent wife through an early admiration for her early novels. He acquired his present position by a long friendship with Philip and a mutual passion for yachting.

Until the King's death which occurred at a time when Browning was fifty-six he was comptroller of Elizabeth's household, a position he had aspired to ever since he heard Elizabeth's inspiring twenty-first birthday speech from South Africa—"That's the person I would like to work for," he said at the time. But it was as a World War II soldier that he became famous.

He commanded the First British Airborne Corps at the Battle of Arnhem in 1944, one of the bitterest engagements of the war. In this action British paratroopers were dropped in a small area around Arnhem, Holland, with the purpose of seizing and holding bridges over the lower Rhine for the main British and American armies advancing from the south. As a project it had the advantage of imagination and novelty, and the disadvantage of being quite impossible. The nearest main force was far too far south to be able to reach the paratroopers before the Germans could recover from their surprise and wipe them out.

However, in true British style the paratroopers fought brilliantly and with sacrificial courage to extricate themselves from a mess they should never have gotten themselves into in the first place. Almost as soon as they hit the ground they were surrounded by Germans who were able to rake the entire landing area with shells. The Germans had the added assistance of considerable quantities of ammunition and supplies which the British and American Air Forces had helpfully dropped for the paratroopers in the wrong places.

Browning had nothing to do with the over-all strategy. He was just there in command of the paratroopers who for days hung on to the bridges they had been ordered to capture, waiting in vain for the arrival of the armies who had been shelled to a standstill to the south.

In the end the Germans swept them from the bridges, confined them inside an ever-decreasing circle, and then overran them. While Daphne du Maurier in her lonely Cornwall mansion listened anxiously by radio, Lord Haw Haw announced triumphantly an "eyewitness" story that Browning had been bayoneted to death in hand-to-hand combat.

As was so often the case with Lord Haw Haw's pronouncements, the truth was somewhat at variance. Browning with a last-organized band of soldiers fought their way out of the German ring, crossed the Rhine by night, and met up with the main forces of the Allied armies some days later. Browning emerged little the worse beyond the crushing need of a civilized gentleman for a hot bath and a shave. The British people who love one brave defeat more than half a dozen resounding victories greeted the exploit ecstatically. "First time I've ever been more famous than my wife," Browning commented complacently.

Today Browning occupies a small cluttered office in the south wing of the Palace, an office decorated with pictures of his beautiful wife, his three children, Tessa, Flavia, and Christian, his terrier, Mouse, and yacht *Jeanne d'Arc*.

He handles Philip's financial business in close co-operation with Lieutenant-Commander "Mike" Parker, Equerry to the Queen, and the Duke of Edinburgh, and Private Secretary to the Duke.

Parker and Browning are vastly different types, but both have in common a long-standing, trusted friendship with Philip. Parker was one of Philip's chums during his wild wartime days in the Far East, and when Philip, in his nervousness before his marriage to Elizabeth, ran his car into a telegraph pole, it was to Parker that he gave it after having it repaired and brightened up.

Parker is an Australian, the first born-and-bred Do-minions man ever to be appointed to such a position. He was born in Melbourne, the son of a captain in the Royal Australian Navy, and educated at Melbourne's Xavier College. He is one of those very rare Australians who has managed to get rid of even the slightest trace of the raw Bowery-Cockney Australian accent; but in many other ways he is Australian to the core. He has an agreeable, coarse

Australian face. He has the Australian knack of picking up every slang expression current in the English-speaking world. His passions are cricket and rugger (the Empire's near-equivalent to American football). His pet hate is pomposity or affectation, and he is on first-name-calling terms with his secretary, his friends, and most of the people who wander into his office in St. James's Palace.

He was thirty-one at the time of the death of King George. Several years before he joined Philip's staff, he had been invalided out of the Royal Navy for stomach trouble, and was actually working inconspicuously for a rope firm in Scotland when Philip called him from London and told him he was marrying Princess Elizabeth.

It has been recorded somewhere that the news made Parker do a perfect Hollywood double-take. It is probable that he did *not* use the old routine and say, "For a moment I thought you said you were marrying Princess Elizabeth." But he certainly said something as ungrammatical as, "You're marrying *who?*" Philip hurriedly went on with the subject and asked him to join his staff as Equerry. Parker accepted on the spot.

Parker is an enthusiastic amateur photographer and his Leica follows him everywhere. He probably has a better collection of informal snaps of Queen Elizabeth and the Duke of Edinburgh than anyone else living. He has not yet reached the position of eminence by which he is awarded a grace-and-favor house—a house leased out tax-free and rent-free by the Monarch to important members of the royal staff—but he does have a pleasant home in fashionable Kensington where he lives with his Scottish wife and two children, Michael and Julie.

Parker's paycheck is now being signed by Brigadier Lord Tryon, who, at the age of forty-five, took over the important job as Keeper of the Privy Purse from sixty-four-year-old Sir Ulick Alexander, Alexander having accepted an Empire business offer in 1952. Tryon is another up-to-date character with a working knowledge of the New World learned in the thirties when he was aide-de-camp to the Governor-General of Canada.

Crown Equerry is Colonel Sir Dermot McMorrough Kavanagh, member of an ancient Irish family. His job is to look after the Queen when she travels. He buys the Buckingham Palace horses, coaches, and automobiles, and was the man chiefly responsible for teaching Elizabeth and Margaret, when they were children, to be such expert horsewomen.

He saved the Coronation arrangements from something of a crisis not long ago by appealing to that race of industrialists always so close to the Irishman's heart, the brewers. Prince Philip and the Duke of Norfolk had a new idea to give all the Empire Prime Ministers a procession of their own. The snag was that there just were not enough coaches and trained horses to go round. Where were they to be found? Answer: in the drink trade which has always been dignified by stables of handsome horses for publicity purposes. The brewers and distillers rallied round Sir Dermot, and he got his horses at no cost to the drinking public.

But the Palace also has a Master of the Horse with quite different duties. He is the Duke of Beaufort who is something of a ceremonial bodyguard. He is responsible for the safety of the Queen while she is in a carriage or on a horse, and he has to ride as close behind her as possible on all occasions to make sure she comes to no harm.

In charge of the domestic arrangements of all the Queen's palaces is Sir Piers "Joey" Legh, Master of the Queen's Household. He is the Palace manager. He drafts dinners and balls, hires and fires the servants required to man the 1,000 rooms at Buckingham Palace, and the few thousand more rooms at the other royal residences. A blunt man who speaks his mind, Legh has the reputation for enjoying an argument and not caring much who it is with.

Legh is one of the few survivors of the old regime of King George VI. The other outstanding one is Sir Alan "Tommy" Lascelles, who must be just about as indispensable to the constitutional functioning of the British Government as it is possible for any one man to be.

Tall, handsome, donnish, dyspeptic, witty, erudite,

and acutely English, Tommy Lascelles is the Queen's Private Secretary, adviser, and go-between. Aged sixty-four at the death of the King, he has always looked younger than his age. It is his job to act as liaison man between the Queen and Number 10 Downing Street, to study the political temper of the moment, and to dig out for the Queen as much intelligence as he can about what is going on behind the scenes in Parliament.

What this means in practice is that Lascelles and Philip are Queen Elizabeth's eyes and ears on the nation, Philip chasing all over the country finding out what the man in the street, on the farm, and down in the mine is thinking, Lascelles keeping to high-level matters of politics and statesmanship.

If a foreign dignitary or a British politician is scheduled to have an interview with the Queen, Lascelles lets her know in advance and in as much detail as he can what will be the subject under discussion. It is vital, above all, that the Queen know everything. Whether she is seeing the Pakistani High Commissioner about some internal Pakistan affair, or the chairman of some big radio electronics convention, she must not appear ignorant or less informed than the person she is talking to, or in any manner less than Queen-size.

This was not so important in the days before nationalism became violent and international suspicions so poisonous. Less than fifty years ago the Kaiser Wilhelm was chatting with Edward VII and said, "Too bad about what's happening in Malta, Eddie."

"Why?" asked the English King blankly. "What's happening in Malta?"

It was probably no issue that might have prevented World War I, but it would never do to confess such ignorance to visitors today.

Lascelles must keep the Queen informed, and accurately informed. He is on first-name terms with every member of the government and every member of the Opposition Front Bench. Officially, as a royal aide Lascelles must be nonpolitical, but as a young man he has the reputation, as Philip had a few years ago, of being somewhat left of center. This probably amounted to no more than a middle-of-the-road liberalism, and it would be nonsense to describe Philip or Lascelles as Socialists. Both are undoubtedly closer to the Conservative Party today than they are to the Laborites.

For the $8,500 which he earns a year Lascelles works a nine- or ten-hour day at the Palace and usually has a thick brief case full of work which he takes home to his grace-and-favor apartment a few yards down the road from Buckingham Palace, in St. James's Palace.

Every morning he talks to diplomats and statesmen

who have appointments with the Queen. When news comes that someone like Winston Churchill wishes to see the Queen, Lascelles is there first to find out what it will be about.

There are only two keys at Buckingham Palace that fit the boxes containing the confidential papers which Elizabeth has to examine or sign. Elizabeth has one and it is Lascelles—not Philip—who holds the other.

Lascelles was educated at Marlborough and Trinity College, Oxford. He won the Military Cross while serving with the Bedfordshire Yeomanry in World War I. It was then that he first developed the dyspepsia which has bothered him ever since—though he does not let it interfere with his enjoyment of good living. He has the casual humor of the English aristocrat, though the only example I can think of at the time of writing is not particularly funny. It shows, at least, an estimable good humor.

Somebody asked him whether he was related to Lord Harewood, whose family name is also Lascelles.

"Oh, yes," he said.

"How?" his companion pressed.

"Most legitimately," he replied.

Why he is called Tommy nobody knows, least of all Tommy himself. Like most of the other officials at Buckingham Palace, he is interested in cricket and fishing, but departs from the rest of the somewhat low-brow Palace set by being strictly long-hair in his taste for music and literature.

As courts go, Elizabeth's and Philip's Court has its virtues and its faults. There are many other officials not mentioned here, most of them excellent fellows and efficient administrators, though one or two suffer from the narrowness of outlook that still afflicts the British nobility. And the Court circle reflects the usual internal frictions, jealousies, animosities, and politics which always thrive in any small, ambitious society.

Yet the internal politics are probably less today than they have been in previous courts. On the whole this is a good, jolly, backslapping Court, more noisy, more brash, and more extrovert than possibly any other Court since the days of the other Queen Elizabeth.

 CHAPTER *ELEVEN*

It is not difficult to discover why it is that Elizabeth and Philip command a world-wide popularity that no politician or movie star can ever hope to enjoy. They love their work. They are outstandingly good-looking. They have handsome children. They are enthusiastic, democratic, ubiquitous, happy, and human, all in an unhappy, undemocratic, and inhuman world.

Many absurd old myths have died since Elizabeth became Queen. Whatever happened, for instance, to the widespread myth that Margaret was the "gay" one of the family and Elizabeth the "serious" one? Nobody ever thinks of that any more. One never sees Elizabeth now but that she appears to be bubbling over with good humor and delight.

Unless an American tourist happens to be in London during August and September when the Royal Family is at Balmoral, he can be reasonably confident of seeing Elizabeth and Philip doing something or other, even if it is merely watching them drive from somewhere important to somewhere else equally important. They go to the theater. They watch the cricket at Lords. They open things, attend things, inaugurate things, lay foundation stones to places, and present prizes to people. They are a part of London life that seems to take London back in time to a better age; and in these times when Englishmen tend to be disillusioned about the present and distrustful of the future, the past takes on a new attraction.

Royalty has not been like this in England for more than a hundred years. Once upon a time the sovereign and his people used to be much closer physically and mentally. Once in history a drunk staggered into a doorway and passed out cold. The doorway happened to be into St. James's Palace and the drunk was awakened by a kick in the ribs delivered by George I himself who was passing by.

A new kinship has grown between royalty and the people. One day in 1952 Elizabeth was touched by a letter addressed to her from Mrs. Edna Springer who had come from Canton, Ohio, to London just to catch a glimpse of her. Mrs. Springer wrote that she had waited outside the Palace gates several times hoping to catch sight of the Queen with no luck. But she intended to go on trying.

To her surprise she received a reply by return of mail. The letter from the Queen's secretary said that if she were at the gates that evening at six forty-five, her mission would be accomplished. Mrs. Springer was there. She had not been standing many minutes when the royal limousine swept soundlessly out of the Palace yard. Inside were the

Queen, Prince Philip, and Princess Margaret, bound for Balmoral. As they passed they all leaned forward and gave the Ohio lady a special wave—a memento of London which she no doubt treasures today far more than any souvenirs of cashmere or Bond Street china.

Nor are Elizabeth and Philip alone among the Royal Family in their attention to the humanities. One evening in November, 1952, a retired businessman named Burnett-Knight was stranded on a country road, swearing at his prewar car that had run out of gasoline, as cars always do, at the exact midpoint between two filling stations, both miles away. As he stood helplessly, a Rolls Royce pulled up alongside, and a middle-aged man in tweeds and a boy, obviously his son, stopped to find out what was the matter.

Burnett-Knight explained, feeling slightly foolish at the sight of his tiny car side by side with this palace on wheels. The man and his son jumped out of the Rolls, linked a piece of rope between the two cars, and took the small one in tow. Twice the rope snapped and the stranger tied it up. The last few yards to the garage they threw away the rope and pushed.

As the retired businessman offered his thanks, the tweedy stranger mumbled something equivalent to the American expression, "You're welcome," and drove off. "And that," explained the garage mechanic, "was the

Duke of Gloucester and young Prince Michael. They do it all the time."

Princess Margaret is just as gracious. She was listed, at a ball, to dance with a young Guardsman who found to his horror that the dance was a polka. "I can't dance a polka, Ma'am," he gasped, crimson. "Don't worry," Margaret laughed, "let's dance something else in polka time."

Elizabeth and Philip do not emerge every day from the Palace, of course. They are often too busy. But even when Londoners do not see their Royal Family, the Royal Family takes many a look at the Londoners. From the window of Buckingham Palace Elizabeth can see her subjects going about their business, crossing the Mall—that most un-English of thoroughfares; resting in St. James's Park—that exotic and most un-English of parks; clustered round the Victoria Memorial in patient hopes of a glimpse of their Queen. It is a pity they cannot see inside and get some idea of what being a Queen involves.

As palaces go, Buckingham Palace cannot be compared to Versailles or Potsdam, which may be one reason why a Queen still rules from Buckingham Palace, and only memories survive in the others. Buckingham Palace is not even as impressive as Greenwich Palace down the Thames, a magnificent place which the British, typically, turned into a hospital for seamen.

But inside this undistinguished nerve center of the

British Empire, a home and a gigantic business enterprise are combined. The summer of 1952 for example found Elizabeth deeply immersed in the business of Queenship. It was a hot summer and the Palace was stuffy and inadequately ventilated.

No air-conditioning cut the heat for the young Queen who sometimes ventured to the front of the Palace for a peep at her people. June 11 and 12 were exceptional days, if only because they were two days in which she was not being pressed quite so hard by official duties, and even found herself with time on her hands. They are worth a closer examination.

An hour before lunch on the eleventh she had changed out of regal costume, handed her jewelry to a maid, and bid a smiling goodday to Douglas Chandor, the American artist who had been commissioned by Mrs. Eleanor Roosevelt to paint her portrait, and returned to the routine work of the day. It was Chandor's first day at the Palace and he would take up several hours of the Queen's time before the portrait was over. But that was part of the business of being royalty, and there were few times in the day at Buckingham Palace when artists and photographers were not at work there.

At that very moment an artist was up in the nursery doing miniatures of Charles and Anne. Elizabeth's engagement pad showed that when Chandor was finished she would be sitting for John Napper who had been commissioned to do her portrait by the Liverpool City Council to lend some color to one of the most dreary Town Halls in England.

This business of sitting for portraits is a chore that many people underestimate. The Queen has a full schedule every day, but court photographers and artists invariably want her to change into ceremonial dress, an act over which most women would spend hours, but which Elizabeth must manage in a few minutes between engagements.

With Chandor satisfied for the time-being, the Queen returned to her office on the garden side of the Palace and was ready at twelve-fifteen to greet His Excellency the Right Honorable V. Krishna Menon, High Commissioner for India, and fifteen minutes later to see her old friend, Professor Lord Cherwell.

Cherwell, born Frederick Lindemann, an Englishman of German parentage, was wartime scientific adviser to Mr. Churchill. He is a vegetarian and a teetotaler, but a man of lavish tastes, notwithstanding, and he has always been close to the Royal Family. His visit at twelve-thirty P.M. was part of a schedule ordered by the Queen as soon as she came to the throne to hold conferences with every member of the cabinet in turn, and for half an hour, Cherwell outlined for her the scientific policies of the Conservative government.

She left her office at one o'clock for lunch, and as she walked through the Palace's creaking art-crammed corridors she could see through the windows London exploding into life in search of food and relaxation. Everywhere below her she could see London's stenographers and office girls blossoming out in summery frocks, eating sandwiches on the benches, while on the grass in the park civil servants from Whitehall spent their hour's break trying to acquire a Riviera tan, their collar-studs unloosened, bowler hats and black jackets on the ground beside them. Around the ornamental lake in the park more of Elizabeth's subjects tossed crumbs to the pelicans and the other exotic birds who live there.

There was no temptation on Elizabeth's part to leave the cares of office and go down and join them. Court advisers agree that she has never sighed for the freedom that cannot be hers.

But heat can oppress even a monarch and Elizabeth must have been relieved that this was proving the slackest working day since she had ascended to the throne four months before. Between now and four P.M. when she had an interview with Georgi Nicolaevitch Zarubin, Russia's ambassador who was retiring to make way for Andrei Gromyko, her appointments all combined pleasure with business.

She and Philip lunched alone together for the first

time in several days. Usually, important guests have to be entertained—French ministers on their way to Washington for conferences, American ministers on their way to Paris for conferences, Commonwealth ministers in London for conferences, or European royalty looking in for a chat. Neither Elizabeth or Philip spoke much during the simple meal, both being absorbed in their respective duties of the day.

Afterward Elizabeth took the elevator, operated by an elderly attendant in the Palace uniform of dark blue, and went up to the second floor where Prince Charles and Princess Anne had just finished their lunch under the fond but keen eyes of Nurse Helen Lightbody. The Queen had a few words with the artist hard at work in a corner, and asked how she was progressing.

"'I think Princess Anne will grow up to look like Princess Margaret, Ma'am," said the artist.

"Yes," commented the Queen, "but Anne, I think, will be taller." At the moment Anne could not have been much smaller, crouched in a small ball, deliriously happy, destroying the castle which Charles had made with his toy bricks. Charles was too absorbed in other matters to notice, though had he spotted what devilry Anne was about he would probably have started an argument.

The sight of their mother was quite a treat for the children, who often did not see her until five in the evening, and not always then. Having matters of importance to discuss, Charles went into conference with his mother and his Nanny. Unlike the cabinet room, the nursery is unconcerned with problems which decide the destinies of mankind or start world wars, but the problems that presented themselves on this occasion were vitally important to the tiny household of a small prince and a baby princess. The issue at hand was Charles' white rabbit.

Should the noble creature be brought to Buckingham Palace or be left at Clarence House, Nurse Lightbody wished to know. At Clarence House the rabbit would miss Charles (at least so Charles established, in the absence of any rebuttal from the rabbit itself). On the other hand it could live at Clarence House a life of lettucy tranquility while at the Palace it was yapped at night and day by Charles' small perpetual-motion corgi, Sugar.

The Queen heard the problem presented objectively by Nurse Lightbody with a few partisan interjections from Charles, and gave her royal command. Bring the rabbit hutch to the Palace, the Queen said, and put it where Charles could play with it while keeping it out of the puppy's way.

Nurse Lightbody had other problems. What to do about Charles' fall wardrobe. The Queen decided on the color of his coats, and whether or not to call the dentist, and who was to come to Anne's second birthday party in

August. Small items for a Queen, but what mother would allow the decisions to be made by anyone else?

And even Charles with his miniature trains and bricks presents some very real problems to Elizabeth. He is Duke of Cornwall, and revenue from the Duchy of Cornwall represents a six-figure fortune which Elizabeth must handle for him until he is eighteen together with the £10,000 ($28,000) a year allotted to him by Parliament. There are questions of when and where Charles is to go to school, and when he will become Prince of Wales, a title reserved for the eldest son of the reigning Monarch.

This is most important. Every English schoolboy knows the story. The Prince of Wales has been the second most important man in England since the days of Edward I who carried out relentless "purifying" wars against the Welsh and the Scots in order to "English-ize" the island. During the war in Wales Edward met the Welsh chiefs at Carnarvon. The chieftains after emerging from a policy conference of their own agreed to Edward's overlordship if he would give them—much nudging, winking, and guffawing here, no doubt—a prince who was born in Wales and spoke neither English nor French. The answer, they thought in delight, would have to be one of themselves. But Edward, with an immortal laugh up his sleeve, lifted up his son, born three days before at Carnarvon, and created the first Prince of Wales.

Because the title of Prince of Wales carries this heavy burden of historic responsibility, and because the Welsh are still rather peeved at being so soundly outsmarted, it is not bestowed automatically like the title of Duke of Cornwall. Charles will be made Prince of Wales when he is old enough to realize that what Edward I did to the Welsh was no laughing matter.

One day Charles will rule, probably as Charles III, though his choice of name also, is not automatic. His grandfather, whose name was Albert, ruled as George VI, and his great-uncle the Duke of Windsor whose name was David ruled as Edward VIII. The reason modern kings seem unable to make up their minds about their first names is simple, though few people know it.

In her will Queen Victoria made a request that all heirs to the throne should include "Albert" in their list of names, but that none should ever reign as "King Albert." Charles has no "Albert" in his name. Philip and Elizabeth broke the royal Victorian tradition when he was christened. Charles could crown himself King Albert or King Rootie Kazootie if he wanted. The choice is his.

All these decisions and conjectures that buzz around the innocent young person of Prince Charles create a condition that Elizabeth and Philip, no matter how they try, cannot treat him exactly like any other child would be treated.

Charles has become used to being saluted by soldiers and cheered by civilians. But thanks to the care of his parents he is growing into a good boy and a good fellow—not necessarily the same thing. The only fault is that, like most of the Windsors, Charles is a trifle shy.

After staying with Charles and Anne for as long as her agenda permitted her, Elizabeth went back to her desk and put a call through on the house phone to Princess Margaret who was entertaining girl friends in her suite at the other end of the Palace. The depth of Margaret's grief after the death of King George VI worried and alarmed Elizabeth and the Queen Mother intensely. Her appetite, always small, went completely. She had nothing to keep her mind busy like her sister, and she was too young and inexperienced to be able to put bereavement in perspective like her mother. At one point she was so ill she needed sedatives to put her to sleep.

"Margaret is a problem child even in her mourning," one friend said sympathetically. Now that Court mourning is over and Margaret is beginning to step out again with a largely new team of boy friends, a weight has lifted from Elizabeth's mind.

The affection between the two sisters is still profound, but now that Elizabeth is Queen, Margaret feels a shyness about calling her at all hours of the day as she used to do, and Elizabeth makes it a point to ring her for a chat whenever she finds herself with a free moment.

Both Margaret and the Queen Mother have settled into a way of living very different from that which they had before the King died. After many delays they moved into their new home at Clarence House shortly before Christmas, 1952, Margaret taking over the four-room suite that was once the nursery of Charles and Anne. She has built in some wall cabinets to hold her collection (large) of American phonograph records, and in the extra space she has found places for her collection (small) of modern novels and collection (medium) of china animals. Her suite is completely self-containing with a small private elevator taking her directly down to an outside door at the side of the house.

The Queen Mother is very contentedly bowing out of the spotlight. She told a friend she considers her primary work done, having educated and raised her daughters, one to the throne. She is dividing her time between her own suite at Clarence House and Barrogill Castle, the home she has bought at the end of nowhere in Scotland. This $40,000 purchase surprised many people who do not realize that the Queen Mother, in spite of her exuberance, has always been a peaceful, reflective person. From the castle which she will inhabit alone, she will be able to see in one direction something like fifteen lighthouses and light buoys scattered among the desolate, rain-pelted islands of the Orkney, and in the other direction, nothing. Just bogs, hills, mists, will o' the wisps, ghosties, and ghoulies.

At Clarence House she is surrounding herself with the flowers she adores, living up to the remark which her mother-in-law, Queen Mary once made, "Betty makes all her rooms into bowers."

The happiness of the rest of the family is a great consolation to the young Queen Elizabeth. So is the support of her husband, Philip, who has described the secret of successful marriage as "a home of one's own and common sense." What it all means is that Elizabeth can throw herself into the business of being a Queen without outside worries.

After talking to Margaret, Elizabeth welcomed Captain Charles Moore, her racing manager, and one of the few persons outside her family with whom she can really relax. Elizabeth has adored horses ever since she was given Peggy, her first Shetland pony, at the age of three. Since she has become Queen they have become a passion and her one mental escape. She has not missed a big race in two years, turning up not only at Ascot and the Epsom Derby but also at Goodwood, which has not been honored with the sovereign's presence since the days of George V. She has even been seen at Hurst Park, a run-of-the-mill course, and at really minor race courses.

Elizabeth is one of those rare race horse lovers who just likes to watch them race. Gambling is quite secondary to her. She does bet, of course; usually from the Palace before the race she asks some friend or other to lay a small bet with one of London's bookmakers. And if that sounds shocking, it should be remembered that bookies in England are not only legal but members of a highly respected profession.

The Queen goes to the paddock to talk to the jockeys between every race, and never goes home until after the last race is run. "Philip's arm is going to be black and blue tonight," one family friend commented during the 1952 flat racing season as she watched the Queen in her excitement pounding Philip's arm at the climax of a close race. Elizabeth was in the paddock talking to Britain's champion jockey, Gordon Richards, at the St. Leger when her three-year-old colt, Gay Time, released from the National Stud, was placed fifth. She stopped by to watch the democratic and totally unfashionable races at Doncaster in Yorkshire. And she was at the Richmond Horse Show to present the Princess Elizabeth Cup to the winner.

Her interview with Captain Moore dealt with some of her stable of horses, after which she was obliged to put thoughts of her favorite hobby aside in time for a conference with the Keeper of the Privy Purse, who signs all checks at Buckingham Palace. By then her "free" time was over and the business of the day was resumed.

At four on the dot the beetle-browed Russian Ambassador Zarubin was ushered in to pay his deadpan respects before departing to inflict himself on the United States as ambassador in Washington. Contrary to general belief, the heads of Western states have very few problems in their dealings with Russian ambassadors. If Moscow has anything important to say, it says it through the Kremlin, or less frequently through its spokesman at the United Nations. For most of the time the ambassadors are never seen at all, but skulk suspiciously in the confines of their embassies. On the rare formal occasions they do emerge, they stick doggedly to the smallest of small talk.

Now, as always, Zarubin in his black morning coat and striped trousers was punctiliously correct. Russians abroad never show the type of national arrogance which moved Joachim Ribbentrop to introduce himself to Edward VIII with a Nazi salute and a "Heil Hitler." Russians on the contrary, probably out of a chronic inferiority complex, always follow protocol to the letter: indeed when King George VI died, correspondents all over the world reported that it was the Soviet flag over the Russian embassies which beat everyone else down to half mast. Zarubin who speaks good English nevertheless relied on the support of an interpreter to present the compliments of the Russian people to Her Majesty, thanked Her Majesty for her hospitality to him, wished with Pecksniffian piety for good relations between Russia and Britain, and expressed his deep regret at having to leave the Court of St. James's where he had been so happy. Elizabeth—her great-uncle, the Tsar of Russia, a man deeply esteemed by her family, had been assassinated by the Bolsheviks—made suitable noises in reply, and Zarubin bowed himself out of the English picture as unobtrusively as he had always appeared in it.

At four-twenty the Earl of Clarendon, now in his last weeks as Lord Chamberlain, was announced and entered carrying a thick sheaf of papers with details of some forthcoming functions which she had to attend. There were also five investitures which she was to hold at the Palace in July, at each of which 350 people had to be decorated. These were the advance details. Later on Elizabeth would get a briefing on every person who was to attend the investiture, a briefing that she would have to study with the greatest of care. It would obviously be a *faux pas* of serious proportions if she were to flub her lines or say the wrong thing to an Army veteran getting a decoration for gallantry in Korea or Malaya; even worse politically if she got her lines wrong with some worthy Socialist official being honored for his services to the trade union movement.

There is no record of Elizabeth ever saying anything wrong. One of her first public functions as Queen was to present the Victoria Cross to Private William Speakman, a six-foot-six-inch giant, for his gallantry in Korea. The fearless Speakman was so nervous at finding himself face to face with the Queen that he was visibly shaking.

Elizabeth said simply as she shook hands, "It is men like you who keep Britain great."

Speakman went red and stammered, "Great honor, Ma'am, great honor."

"Yes," smiled Elizabeth, "a great honor, for me."

That is typical of Elizabeth's tact. Every adviser in the Palace has commented also on her efficiency. There are many examples of her sureness of touch, but one is the way she prepares her schedule for official visits. It is the Queen's privilege and responsibility to decide just how long she will spend touring a hospital, a school, or a factory, and she knows to a minute how long it takes to do what. As a result her visits always go without a hitch. Nothing is skimped, and school children who may have waited for hours for the big thrill of seeing the Queen always get a good look at her.

This is no small matter. Kings and Queens do not need votes and it loses them nothing if they don't do their job properly, but it causes deep disappointment among people who have waited to see them.

The writer of this book remembers, as a small boy, turning out with the rest of his school and the rest of the village to see one of the members of the Royal Family drive through. Everyone was in his Sunday best. The heat was killing and perspiration was running in rivers down the schoolboys lined up at the front of the crowds. After what seemed like hours, and was certainly at least one hour because the teachers themselves were becoming fractious, a covered limousine flashed past at high speed and was gone before anyone could even wave a flag. That was that.

Elizabeth would never dream of being so highhanded with her subjects' affections. Her schedules always go off perfectly and local officials are never left with a ghastly five minutes overhanging, a Queen on their hands, and nothing left to show her.

It is not easy to dove tail details of official visits to such a fine point. Princess Margaret has given plenty of officials gray hairs, once or twice by her own fault, though more often through circumstances beyond her control. At one time she had a bad reputation for canceling appearances on rather trivial grounds, disappointing many people. But it was the delicacy of her position and through no fault of hers that at least one board of directors got the jitters. Margaret was due to visit a northern factory one day in 1952, and the directors had a sudden panic. What, they asked, would they offer her for refreshment?

"Isn't she always supposed to be going out to night clubs?" the chairman asked. "Well, let's cover every eventuality. Let's get champagne, dry martinis, wet martinis, scotch, wine, and—oh yes—she's supposed to be interested in America, better get some Coca-Cola."

It was a highly successful visit. Margaret looked adorable. Everybody loved her. She loved everybody. At the end the chairman invited her to the board room and confidently asked her what she would care for in the way of refreshment.

"Thank you," Margaret said, smiling sweetly. "May I have a cup of tea, please?"

Which only goes to show that entertaining royalty is a complicated business. Elizabeth's instinct in these matters is not only sounder than either her father's or the rest of her family's; it is more reliable even than such experienced advisers as the Earl of Clarendon or Sir Alan Lascelles who have been arranging such things for years. One adviser remonstrated respectfully when she allowed herself an hour to be present at a dedication. "That will leave you no time to rest before your next appointment, Ma'am."

"It can't be helped," the Queen replied. "I shall have to rest before or afterward."

When the Earl of Clarendon gathered up his papers at four forty-five Elizabeth found herself with the unusual prospect of an evening almost free. It was so early that the

Mall was not yet alive with the taxis and automobiles which every evening take Londoners to Chelsea, Kensington, Chiswick, and residential points west. From now on Elizabeth had nothing to do except her homework.

While she played with Charles and Anne in the nursery from five to six P.M., the "boxes" which have plagued British Kings and Queens for centuries were being placed by attendants on her desk in her apartments in the Belgian Suite on the ground floor (King George VI's suite is now empty and will probably remain so for as long as the Queen Mother lives). When she goes for week ends to Sandringham the boxes get there ahead of her, and they overtake her on her trips to Balmoral. They follow her to the races and are waiting for her when she gets back from an evening at the theater.

With the boxes disposed of, locked up by a tubular key, and returned via dispatch rider to Whitehall, only one task remained on the evening under examination before she went to dress for dinner with her husband. *Hansard*, British equivalent of the *Congressional Record*, had to be read from beginning to end. As Queen, Elizabeth is no longer allowed to enter Parliament, except for the formal State opening every year. Only from *Hansard* does she learn what is going on, with Sir Alan Lascelles filling her in with interpretive, nonpolitical comments. It is a chore but it could be worse.

Nobody filibusters in the House of Commons the way they do from time to time in the American Senate, so nobody reads out of telephone directories in order to keep the floor. The standard of debate in the Commons therefore tends to be on a higher level and usually makes for good reading, even when tempers fray and Opposition members refer to Mr. Churchill as a "goose," as they did once in 1952.

After *Hansard* the day's work is done. The Queen puts on an evening dress, and Philip usually wears a dinner jacket even when they dine alone; invariably when they have company. Together they discuss the topics that interest all married couples, children, home, vacations, and the business of the day. Philip often gives Elizabeth an outline of some speech he is planning to make, and Elizabeth listens with deep respect.

Philip's gift for speeches has impressed and influenced Elizabeth profoundly, and, within the limits of what a monarch can and cannot say, she has tried to emulate him in writing her own speeches and finding her own phrases.

Some of Philip's 1952 speeches were excellent. To the Chamber of Commerce and Manufacturers in Edinburgh he appealed for "enterprise, enthusiasm, and hard work," and quoted from philosopher Bertrand Russell, "America has invented the phrase Yes-men for those who flatter great executives. In England we are more troubled by No-men who make it their business to employ clever ignorance in opposing and sabotaging every scheme suggested by those who have energy, imagination, and enterprise.

"I am afraid our No-men are a thousand times more harmful than the American Yes-men. If we are to recover prosperity we shall have to find ways of emancipating energy and enterprise from the frustrating control of constitutionally timid ignoramuses.

"There is a school of thought," Philip continued forcefully, "which says 'what was good enough for my father is good enough for me.' I have no quarrel with this sentiment at all, so long as it is not made an excuse for stagnation, frustration, and inefficiency, and I am quite sure our fathers would be the first to agree with this. The great name of British commerce was founded on honesty, fair dealing, and hard work. But do not forget that the great position of British industry was won when we led the world in inventive imagination and the spirit of adventure."

Philip is usually good for a laugh somewhere in the course of a speech. One night before a naval audience which included nineteen admirals, he replied to a toast of "The Younger Seafarers." It was proposed by the dinner

233

president, the ferocious Vice Admiral Sir Gilbert Stephenson, wartime head of training for naval operations in the Western Approaches.

Philip, though only a commander, was not a bit put out by the scintillation of gold lace that surrounded him—so different from the bashful young Prince of a few years before. He told the diners he was attending "under false pretences" because he had served in East Coast convoys during the war, and not in the Western Approaches at all. Then, rolling a Groucho Marx eye round the guests, he said condescendingly, "Still, we did actually hear about you, and understood you did quite well."

"Mike" Parker, one of Philip's old shipmates, almost went over backward in the general laughter.

One topic above all that fascinates both Elizabeth and Philip is sports. They must be two of the most sports-mad couples in the world, and Elizabeth listened for hours, probably in some envy, to the stories Philip told her about his visit to Helsinki for the Olympic Games. As in other things they are officially presumed to be nonpartisan. If either of them attend international sports competitions they behave with careful neutrality, but together they don't bother to hide the fact that they are all out for England, and were disappointed that Great Britain did not win more prizes at Helsinki, even though British athletes did better than was expected.

234

ELIZABETH *and* PHILIP

On one miserable night in the history of British sports
Philip, immaculate in dinner jacket, went to Harringay to
watch a spectacular boxing bill. Five British fighters were
matched against five foreign fighters and all but one of the
home boys lost. The worst upset was when Don Cockell,
British and European lightheavyweight champion—a young
bruiser on whom Britain had squandered a prodigious over-
optimism—was walloped senseless by an almost unknown
American named Jim Slade. Philip looked as depressed as
the rest of the crowd that left the arena.

But there is one thing common to sports fans all over
the world. The defeat of their home team does not make
them lose interest, and the enthusiasm of Philip and Elizabeth never flags. "It makes life so much easier for us the
way the Queen and the Duke enjoy sport," one court official admitted. "Royalty has to be present at all major
sporting occasions, and they would have a dull time otherwise. Oddly enough there is only one sport which does not
interest either of them too much, and that is tennis. And
fortunately we have the Duchess of Kent who loves it, and
she usually does the honors at Wimbledon."

Elizabeth's love of horse racing is greater than Philip's. Philip prefers other sports, but since Elizabeth has
known him and come under his influence, she has developed, as a good wife should, an appreciation of the many
sports at which Philip excels. Since her marriage Elizabeth

235

has become a keen fan of cricket, yachting, athletics, and polo, all games at which Philip is outstanding, and both of them follow the progress of soccer and rugby, England's rival winter sports.

Cricket is, or was, Philip's top game. His own play at one time not long ago was of good Minor-Counties standard, which is roughly approximate to International League baseball: in other words the standard just below the top. Unfortunately Philip has not had time to keep up the practice which this subtle and intricate game demands, and one or two of his performances in the past couple of years have been pretty dreadful.

But his enthusiasm for the game is overwhelming. A South African cricket writer told this correspondent in 1952, "When South Africa sent a cricket team to England in 1947, it was murder trying to explain the finer points of the game to Princess Elizabeth. She was very charming, of course, just as she always is. She wasn't married then, and she hardly knew the difference between the batsman and the square-leg umpire. When we came back to England in 1951, though, my word what a difference. *She* was telling *us!*"

We have now meandered through Elizabeth's duties on June 11, 1952. For the sake of balance and comparison, this more briefly, is what happened next day.

A sound sleep, the blessing which comes of superb

good health and mental equipoise, and Elizabeth rose alert but not too willingly at seven A.M. This is an hour earlier than she used to do when she was a Princess, and illustrates the fact that even a Queen, and even a Queen of Elizabeth's strength of mind, must sometimes yield to the inevitable. Since she has ascended the throne Elizabeth has been forced from two firmly announced positions.

First, she was determined to stick to her accustomed time of rising, and, secondly, to devote every evening from five to six P.M. to her children. But she quickly found that rules must sometimes be broken. She now finds a seven A.M. rising essential, and is often obliged to cut short though seldom cut out altogether her children's hour.

Breakfast for the Queen is ample and English, consisting of fruit juice, bacon, and egg, or an omelet, or that breakfast treat which so antagonized our South African friend in the first chapter and which chokes all except alley cats and Englishmen, a kipper. While she eats Elizabeth listens to the eight A.M. news on the BBC.

On her desk the secretary has laid two or three of the leading London and provincial newspapers. These she reads with concentration, not sticking to the items of special interest marked by the secretary. She begins with the front page, then turns to the editorials, and then to the sports pages, lightly skimming the inside pages.

Then the round begins again, starting with the conference on future business which she conducts from her arm-chair with Sir Alan Lascelles. She dictates her correspond-ence which usually amounts to about fifty letters a day. Both Elizabeth and Princess Margaret have been obliged to start sending all private letters by registered mail because so many of their letters have been pilfered somewhere along the line and sold to souvenir hunters for large sums.

During the morning she will probably see Lieutenant Colonel Martin Charteris who was her secretary when she was a Princess and is now one of the assistant private sec-retaries. Lascelles and Charteris brief her on the various matters likely to need her attention today. This being June 12 there was a break at eleven A.M. for a visit to Charles and Anne, and then, at midday a series of special appointments.

The first was with the small, black-robed figure of Mrs. Ernest Bevin, widow of the Socialist Foreign Secretary who died in 1951. Elizabeth had a decoration to give her but did not want to leave it until the July investitures, because the Queen for many years had admired the irascible old Foreign Secretary, and the two women, one recently de-prived of a famous father, and the other of a famous hus-band, were left alone together for fifteen minutes.

Elizabeth would probably have liked this meeting to run longer, but the schedule was too tight, and at twelve-fifteen she had an appointment with an old friend, Walter

Elliott, former Conservative Minister of Agriculture, whom she made a Companion of Honor. At twelve-thirty it was the turn of Osbert Peake, Minister of National Insurance in the Conservative Government, to bring her up to date on what was happening in the insurance business these days.

Finding herself without a business lunch date for the second day in a row Elizabeth called Princess Margaret and the sisters arranged to lunch together, but before she could leave the office, she had some business to finish off with the Vice Chamberlain of the Queen's Household, Henry Studholme; and with the Government whip, Patrick Buchan-Hepburn, who had hurried from the House of Commons with a bill for her to sign.

In the afternoon she had a presentation party for a couple of hundred debutantes from all over the world, a small handful coming from the United States. Back at her office she knighted a departing ambassador, checked on forthcoming business with "Tommy" Lascelles, saw the children between five and six, heard Winston Churchill's weekly report, had another financial hassle with the Keeper of the Privy Purse, Sir Ulick Alexander, spent a couple of hours on the boxes, then went to her suite to bathe and dress for dinner with Philip.

These have been a couple of quiet days for the Queen. When visiting royalty turns up from Europe, and when the dignitaries arrive from the latest international deadlock, things really look busy inside the big square palace, particularly if Elizabeth has any extra tasks to attend to as she does in the summer, practicing to perfect her side saddle riding for the big Trooping of the Color ceremony on her official birthday. (Her actual birthday is April 21, but the outdoor celebrations are customarily held in June out of a well-founded distrust of the English weather.)

There is no escape from official duties at Windsor or Sandringham. The foreign dignitaries are just as happy there as they are at Buckingham Palace, and stay for week ends, interspersing their talks on the subject of world peace with little safaris into the woods in search of pheasants to shoot.

But Elizabeth lightens her tasks with a sense of humor that is all her own. One evening in 1952 she went to the theater with a party of friends to see *The Young Elizabeth*, a play about the Queen's great predecessor. During the course of the play one of the royal courtiers in the Palace says, "There are too many people in this house," which would not have struck most people as a funny line, but which Elizabeth greeted with a gurgle of merriment, for reasons not difficult to deduce.

The one factor which impresses any observer of the Queen's activities is the almost complete absence of spare time even on her holidays. "Anyone can be a King," a court adviser commented to a friend, in different words. "All a King has to do is be a King. But a Queen has to be a King, a Queen, a mother, a housekeeper, a business woman, a landlord, and a wife."

On a typical day in the summer of 1952 when Elizabeth visited Ascot to relax at the races, she had to grant audience to the Mayor, Dean, and Chapter of St. George's Chapel, Windsor; the Duke of Norfolk, her land agent at Sandringham, and her trainer, both of whom have been mentioned in the Honors List. She gave a house party that week end, and when all the guests had gone to bed, she settled down to the boxes that had followed her from London.

At Buckingham Palace today everyone chips in to do what he can to help Elizabeth; Philip, as we have seen, shouldering an immense amount of work and impatient to shoulder more; the Queen Mother attending to special functions and making a specialty of flower shows; the Princess Royal, sister of the late King, specializing in the activities of Girl Guides (English for Girl Scouts); Princess Margaret performing hard and heroically at presentations and other tasks, and at the same time supplying the glamour and the light relief.

Yet Elizabeth is left with a quantity and a complication of problems which few people realize. Even an item like her wardrobe is vastly more involved than it ever was for the King, who could use the same suits for years, and, when in doubt, close his eyes and pull out a uniform. Elizabeth has to dress for every occasion with great care, knowing the critical and not overkind eyes are fixed on every detail of her clothes.

In her position she cannot get away from it all for a few days with a trip to Paris or the Riviera. Elizabeth takes two months' holiday every year—most years at Balmoral—and her chief relaxation is when she goes on after-dinner fishing expeditions with Philip. But at Balmoral Elizabeth is reminded of the fact that she is a landlord and an employer of 250 people, and has to start thinking about maintaining her castles, stables, relatives, and a staff which includes in either honorary or paid capacity Yeomen of the Guard, an Honorable Corps of Gentlemen-at-Arms, Aides-de-Camp, Equerries, Ladies of the Bedchamber, Maids of Honor, and huddles of footmen, electricians, maids, night watchmen, etc.

Yet we have already seen that the burden of the monarchy will never have the terrible physical consequences on Queen Elizabeth that it had on her father, because Elizabeth so much enjoys everything about her job, and her work is her play.

More nagging than any issue of the Queen's immediate health seems to be the doubt that many people, Americans especially, cannot help feeling about the purpose of a monarchy in a present-day world. What, they ask, does it prove for a King who is a figurehead to kill himself through overwork; what, in the equivalent British slang, is it all in aid of?

Ardent royalists—and the English Crown has few enemies either at home or abroad—are always indignant at the very slightest suggestion that it is unnecessary, then they always reply to the charge with the wrong answers.

The monarchy *is* necessary, and positively indispensable to Britain and the Commonwealth, because without it there would be no Commonwealth, and possibly no Britain worth mentioning.

The strength of the British monarchy is in its lack of positive power. The fate of Farouk and Leopold shows what happens to political kings. This has always been basic and well understood, yet Elizabeth's accession in a troubled world in February, 1952, started a world-wide daydream of a new, virile monarchy that would provide the leadership which the free world seemed so conspicuously to lack.

The newspapers, not only of Britain but also of the United States and the Commonwealth, were full of excitement at the prospects of a wonderful new Elizabethan age. It was all quite nonsense, of course. How the Queen was expected to perform the miracle nobody ventured to say. That presumably was *her* problem. The madness has dissipated since then though the Coronation has tended to revive it. But there is little feeling left of a great new, feminine influence in world affairs who by a stroke of a magic wand, would eliminate communism, wipe out taxes, reduce apartment rentals, and provide free beer for the aged and infirm.

Of course Elizabeth has not proved herself a leading figure in the world. She has not presented the West's case in person before the United Nations, nor led an attack like Boadicea against the West's enemies. No Boadicea, as *Time* magazine would say, she. She has not disbanded the fighting forces, sold the Royal Navy to the nation's scrap merchants, dissolved Parliament, or any of the other misty, theoretical rights which a monarch is supposed to have. Think of the devil there would be to pay if she tries. The British remain in their usual mess. Rationing persists well into Elizabeth's reign, and conditions are just as severe.

Yet the British monarchy still does a first-class job for the world. Elizabeth will reign for fifty years and more, and well inside that period Elizabeth will establish herself for posterity as a world figure to stand up with statesmen and presidents.

Without the Queen, the Commonwealth which is the one great third force in the world, now happily allied to America, would disintegrate. And above all power considerations the English Crown gives the final form and shape to its own age. Gladstone can bequeath a bag, Chamberlain an umbrella, and Hoover a depression, but there is no such thing as a Churchillian age or a Rooseveltian age. The expressions sound strange and foreign on the tongue. Only an English King or Queen can put a stamp on an entire age as did Elizabeth I, Charles II, Anne, George I, II, and III, Victoria, and Edward VII. The only reason the reigns of George V and George VI did not become in any way "Georgian" or "neo-Georgian" was because those two men were not dynamic enough in their kingship. All the facilities are there, the symbolism, the inspiration, the non-controversial leadership; only the personalities fell short.

Already one can feel the impact of Elizabeth's personality, in America faintly, in England very strongly. Tangibly she has stimulated the greatest national interest in horse racing since the days of Edward VII, and there has been new energy in the horse-breeding business, a valuable dollar-earning enterprise in Britain. In the fashion world the Elizabethan impact has been noted, too. Experts agreed that the London styles of 1952 were a noticeable improvement on the past. This could not be directly due to Elizabeth whose clothes sense is still uncertain, but it is obviously inspired by the presence of a lovely young Queen on the throne of England.

Horse racing, horse-breeding, and fashion are not too important but they are as good a start as any for a Queen whose reign can still be counted easily in months.

The British sovereign also has an important political influence. He has the right constitutionally "to encourage, advise, and warn" the Prime Minister in his policies. If this does not seem much of a remnant to survive from the old Divine Right of Kings, it can still be effective.

As recently as November, 1951, King George VI stirred up an argument over his political activities. Earl Mountbatten in a speech to the Rotarians in London, admitted this.

"When Mr. Attlee asked me to go to India as Viceroy, I at first told him that my answer was no. I said that nobody in his right frame of mind would dream of going out to try and solve an insoluble problem.

"I then found that His Majesty himself was sold on the idea, and it was the King who next asked me to take on the job. I am sure you will agree that once the King asks you to do a job, nobody can say no. So I took it."

In other words, the man who finally settled the chronic Indian question did it directly for the King and not for the Prime Minister. But it worried the *Financial Times*, English equivalent of the *Wall Street Journal*. "It is surprising," the *Times* commented uneasily, "that a member of the Board of Admiralty who is also a relation of His

Majesty should have treated the Rotary Club to an account of the King's participation in a political appointment which swiftly terminated the long and glorious history of the Anglo-Indian Empire." That was a comparatively small matter. British affairs need only have taken a very slightly different turn in 1952 for Elizabeth to have had a first-rate political crisis dropped right in her lap. Suppose that Churchill had retired (as many critics had been urging him to do), and Anthony Eden had become Prime Minister (as he probably would have done). Then suppose Eden, already divorced, had announced his intention to remarry (as he did).

Think of the moral clamor that might have arisen. It rumbled quite loud even as things stood when Eden married Clarissa Churchill, the Prime Minister's niece. But if Eden himself had been Prime Minister instead of Foreign Secretary, and responsible to a Queen who would not have been a Queen anyway if her uncle had not finished up on the wrong side in a battle over divorce, a major crisis might have developed, with every prejudice in religious history turning up to have its say. If the crisis were severe enough, it might then have fallen on Elizabeth, alone and twenty-six years old, to decide whether Eden should or could remain Prime Minister. If Eden went, to whom could she turn?

Any decision would be hers alone, and whatever it

turned out to be it would be of critical importance to the whole free world, with Washington, London, and Paris involved and the whole democratic alliance affected.

There is great strength and triumph in Queen Elizabeth. When the birth of Prince Charles was announced to a party of Elizabeth's friends and relatives in 1948, someone stopped the cheering and said, "We cheer as though we are surprised. We should have known Elizabeth would have a prince. She never lets us down."

When the King died, Elizabeth came to Sandringham and laid a wreath on his coffin. It was a white circle of lilies of the valley, camellias, hyacinths, and carnations, and tied to it was the farewell dedication, "To darling Papa, from your loving and devoted daughter and son-in-law, Lilibet, Philip."

Since February, 1952, Elizabeth has changed and grown. Churchill commented on her not long after her succession, "There is too much care on that young brow."

But the great old man was being less wise than usual. The Queen Mother showed sounder insight a few days after Elizabeth became Queen. "Somehow," she said, "we are not afraid."